HISTORIC HOUSES OF PARIS

RESIDENCES OF THE AMBASSADORS

EXECUTIVE EDITOR
Suzanne Tise-Isoré

EDITORIAL COORDINATION
Aurélie Hagen-Bastelica

EDITORIAL ASSISTANT
Joy Sulitzer

GRAPHIC DESIGN
Bernard Lagacé

TRANSLATED FROM THE FRENCH BY
David Radzinowicz

PROOFREADING
Helen Woodhall

PRODUCTION
Élodie Conjat-Cuvelier

COLOR SEPARATION
Les Artisans du Regard, Paris

PRINTED BY
Graphart, Trieste

Simultaneously published in French as *Demeures historiques,
les résidences d'ambassadeurs à Paris*.
© Flammarion SA, Paris, 2010

English-language edition
© Flammarion SA, Paris, 2010

Flammarion SA
87, quai Panhard et Levassor
75647 Paris Cedex 13
France

editions.flammarion.com

Dépôt légal: 10/2010
10 11 12 3 2 1
ISBN: 978-2-08-030148-2
Printed in Italy by Graphart

HISTORIC HOUSES OF PARIS

RESIDENCES OF THE AMBASSADORS

ALAIN STELLA

PHOTOGRAPHY BY FRANCIS HAMMOND

Flammarion

ASSOCIATION
BIENVENUE
EN FRANCE

Contents

7   Foreword

8   THE QUAI D'ORSAY   FRENCH MINISTRY OF FOREIGN AND EUROPEAN AFFAIRS

28   HÔTEL DE BESENVAL   SWISS CONFEDERATION

44   HÔTEL D'ESTRÉES   RUSSIAN FEDERATION

60   HÔTEL DE BEAUHARNAIS   FEDERAL REPUBLIC OF GERMANY

86   HÔTEL D'AVARAY   KINGDOM OF THE NETHERLANDS

100   HÔTEL DE CHAROST   UNITED KINGDOM OF GREAT BRITAIN AND NORTHERN IRELAND

122   HÔTEL DE LA ROCHEFOUCAULD-DOUDEAUVILLE   ITALIAN REPUBLIC

142   HÔTEL DE LA MARCK   KINGDOM OF BELGIUM

156   HÔTEL DE MONACO   REPUBLIC OF POLAND

174   HÔTEL DE PONTALBA   UNITED STATES OF AMERICA

192   HÔTEL DE BÉHAGUE   ROMANIA

214   HÔTEL LANDOLFO-CARCANO   STATE OF QATAR

226   HÔTEL BERTHIER DE WAGRAM   KINGDOM OF SPAIN

244   HÔTEL LAFONT DE LA VERNÈDE   REPUBLIC OF PERU

256   HÔTEL EPHRUSSI   ARAB REPUBLIC OF EGYPT

270   HÔTEL PILLET-WILL   JAPAN

284   HÔTEL DE ROUVRE   PEOPLE'S REPUBLIC OF CHINA

302   HÔTEL D'OROSDI   REPUBLIC OF ARGENTINA

312   HÔTEL DE LOTA   REPUBLIC OF CÔTE D'IVOIRE

320   HÔTEL DE LA TOUR D'AUVERGNE   REPUBLIC OF CHILE

330   HÔTEL DE LÉVY   PORTUGUESE REPUBLIC

348   HÔTEL DE MARLBOROUGH   REPUBLIC OF INDIA

362   RESIDENCE OF THE AMBASSADOR   COMMONWEALTH OF AUSTRALIA

372   Bibliography

373   Acknowledgments

374   Index

FACING PAGE *The Hôtel de Béhague's library, of oval form, with paneling from the eighteenth century.*

Foreword

THIS SPLENDID VOLUME IS THE RESULT OF THE FRUITFUL COLLABORATION BETWEEN a publisher, an author, and a photographer on the one hand, and the association "Bienvenue en France" on the other. Without the creative input of the former and the talent for opening doors of the latter, *Historic Houses* would never have been possible and some of the most glorious but least-known interiors in Paris would have remained forever hidden from the public eye.

Centered on discovery, access, and involvement, "Bienvenue en France," which I founded in 1979, is predicated on the idea that friendship should transcend both borders and diplomatic interests. From the very first, it was accredited and supported by the French Ministry of Foreign Affairs, which grasped the fact that cordial, even friendly, relations that bring individuals and, beyond them, whole peoples closer together, are no less important than a professional dialog.

In a world capital like Paris, with its numerous diplomatic missions, an association that encourages international interaction is no luxury. Its remit is to see that no country feels ostracized and that every member of staff in an embassy, whatever its place in the diplomatic hierarchy, receives a welcome worthy of the great French tradition of hospitality. Since its establishment, the many female French volunteers belonging to "Bienvenue en France" have laid on countless activities for its members, with the intention that our guests learn more about our country, including our language, and experience everyday life in a French household. In this way, not only do they become fond of France and start to appreciate its values, but, in exchange, our visitors offer glimpses of their home country, opening the eyes of their hosts to new customs and lifestyles, even to a different culture.

This year "Bienvenue en France" is celebrating its thirtieth birthday. Every year some four hundred female diplomats and their partners of more than a hundred nationalities join its ranks, staying on for an average of three years. Of every religion and from every tradition, its members are catered for by over one hundred and fifty women, who organize for them a host of activities, from language and literature courses to an introduction to French cuisine and gastronomy, as well as visits to museums, exhibitions, monuments, and companies, and lectures, concerts, and creative workshops. Beyond, and sometimes in spite of, the diplomatic tensions that may arise between governments, through these regular activities, enduring bonds have been woven and long-term friendships born. With subtlety and discretion, "Bienvenue in France" is, in this respect, an instrument for mutual understanding and peace.

From the very outset, ambassadors to Paris have been pleased to open their residences to the members of "Bienvenue en France." These are buildings that number among the most elegant private dwellings in the capital, *hôtels particuliers* built over the centuries that have passed through the hands of members of royal and imperial families, aristocrats, and wealthy industrialists.

These sumptuously appointed abodes are not only beautiful residences; they are also a focus for intense diplomatic activity. Often better than in the chancellery itself, here, at a reception or around a table with some fine food, the ice is broken and bonds forged, allowing business to proceed more smoothly and agreements to be finalized more speedily. In addition to presenting their breathtaking decors and the interesting events they stage, this book also seeks to cast light on the key roles played by these outposts. Aided and abetted by the team assembled by Flammarion, it has, however, only seen the light of day due to the "open sesame" quality of "Bienvenue in France" and the warm and friendly relations we enjoy.

This book is also intended as a tribute to those many nations with representations in France that do so much to preserve their "homes." The manner in which they respect what are often jewels of our architectural heritage, maintaining them in accordance with French rules and regulations, is greatly to their honor.

Now, as I turn the pages of this gorgeous volume with its generous selection of official residences from every period occupied by diplomats from every continent, my abiding impression is that our goal has indeed been achieved. ❧

FACING PAGE *Glimpse of the Music Room from the hall on the first floor in the Hôtel de Beauharnais.*

Marie-Thérèse FRANÇOIS-PONCET
Founding president, Bienvenue en France

THE QUAI D'ORSAY

FRENCH MINISTRY OF FOREIGN
AND EUROPEAN AFFAIRS

THE QUAI D'ORSAY

FRENCH MINISTRY OF FOREIGN AND EUROPEAN AFFAIRS

Construction date 1844–53

Architect Jacques Lacornée

EAST OF THE INVALIDES ESPLANADE DOWN THE SEINE, THE QUAI D'ORSAY BORDERS the vast and exquisite garden of the Chamber of Deputies. When the French government decided to build the Ministry for Foreign Affairs on the site in 1844 the project was entrusted to a well-known architect who had already designed the Palais d'Orsay situated a few hundred meters farther on: Jacques Lacornée (1779–1856). After a series of political and economic setbacks, the as yet unfinished building was finally taken over by the Ministry in 1853. The works, however—particularly in respect of the interior decoration—were to continue for many years to come.

This period witnessed the triumph of the Napoleon III style, an eclectic amalgam of all the major French decorative idioms. The Ministry bears all its hallmarks: its long neoclassic frontage with columns conceals two floors of halls, dining rooms, offices, and apartments whose glorious decor amounts to a beauty pageant in which the styles of the Renaissance, Louis XV, Louis XVI, and the Empire follow on from each other in quick succession. So opulent is it that an Austrian ambassador, visiting in 1854, called it a "sumptuous and almost presumptuous palace."

It is true that these enfilades, where chapters of world history were—indeed still are being—written, are awash with gold, carvings, and stucco, with cornices, piers, and overdoors, whose gleam vies with the glimmer from innumerable chandeliers. One's abiding sensation on visiting the two reception floors would be one of oppression, were it not for the light scattering of masterpieces and the many mute witnesses to crucial events in French history.

Important visitors and heads of state are greeted in the vestibule to the west, at the ceremonial entrance to the building where the great staircase soars, with one of the majestic full-length portraits of the Cardinal de Richelieu painted by Philippe de Champaigne.

In the first hall, known as the Anteroom of the Ushers (Antichambre des Huissiers) stands the great canvas by Édouard Dubufe representing a session at the 1856 Congress of Paris that put an end to the Crimean War. The actual sittings of the Congress were held in the Salon of the Ambassadors a few yards farther on. Today one can also admire two eighteenth-century Gobelins tapestries after cartoons by the Flemish painter Lucas van Leyden.

Continuing eastward down the side of the building facing the Seine, one arrives in the vast Clock Room (Salon de l'Horloge), with its magnificent gold embellishments, that owes its name to the horological masterwork set into the mantelpiece, itself surmounted by an allegorical sculpture representing France as a figure of Liberty.

For a century and half, these walls patrolled by Ionic pilasters, this richly ornamented ceiling of cherubs and garlands of gilt between allegories of the Four Continents painted on the overdoors, gazed down on many important functions, some purely festive, others more diplomatic. Several august bodies have met here, such as the Inter-Allied Conference of 1917 and the Peace Conference of 1919, and it has witnessed events such as the signing of the Kellogg-Briand Pact in 1928 and the creation of the European Coal and Steel Community in 1950, an agreement that laid the foundation for the European Community.

After this historic hall, the great dining room running crosswise gives onto the garden to the south. In this room, beneath eight chandeliers, dinner and luncheon functions are given on the occasion of State or other official visits. These number at most ten or so a year, served at small tables of eight to ten diners according to a table plan diligently devised by the head of protocol.

At the Quai d'Orsay, all the dishes—in venerable Sèvres china—are prepared on the spot . . . except for the bread. The kitchens have a staff of about a dozen working under the orders of a *chef de cuisine* and a *chef pâtissier*. Larger official functions also require a

fair number of extras. The kitchen personnel is geared into action on many other occasions: working lunches served in the dining rooms on the first floor, as well as breakfasts and evening receptions. The magnificent decoration of the Quai d'Orsay should not make us forget that here people are busy thinking and acting in the service of French foreign policy. Staff work here every day from morning to night: the offices of the minister and his secretariat, on the garden front, are constantly abuzz, and the salons on both floors are transformed regularly into meeting rooms.

Until 1973, the first storey and its fifteen or so rooms were intended to receive official guests to France. That year, the king of Spain, Juan Carlos, was the last such to be accommodated in the palace. Ever since, exalted visitors have been lodged in the Hôtel de Marigny, while the floor above, just as sumptuously decorated as the one below it, has become a place for meetings and work.

Even the so-called "King" and "Queen" rooms, where a great number of sovereigns and heads of State and their wives have stayed, have been converted into conference rooms, while keeping their original decoration. The two wonderful bathrooms attached to these chambers offer the only examples of modern decoration in the Quai d'Orsay: of an art deco style, all lacquer and glass, they were designed in 1938 by the architect Pierre Bruneau in collaboration with the decorators Auguste Labouret and Jacques Adnet, on the occasion of a visit by the British sovereigns. The bathtubs and hand basins are in gold mosaic for the king and in silver for the queen. They were completely restored in 2003 and 2004.

It is not uncommon to find unique historical documents or artworks displayed in the salons of the ground floor, relating to the history of France, Europe, and the world: royal edicts, peace treaties, military and commercial treaties housed in the diplomatic archives. Not far from the display cases containing centuries of France's collective memory, today's history is being written page by page. ❖

BELOW *A gilt-bronze female head set into the mantelpiece in the gallery of Peace adjacent to the Clock Room.*
FACING PAGE *The Clock Room. The clock by bronze-founder Victor Paillard (1805–1886) that gave its name to a room formerly known as the Festival Room (Salon des Fêtes) because of the dazzling masked balls and concerts held here during the Second Empire. An allegory of France, signed by Joseph Michel Ange Pollet (1814–1873), strides forward amid a flower-and-fruit decor carved by Liénard.*

PRECEDING PAGES *General view of the "Napoleon III" decor in the Clock Room. Since 1917, a great number of international treaties have been signed beneath a ceiling painted by François Nolau (1804–1883) and Auguste Alfred Rubé (1815–1899) and adorned by twelve cherubs carved by the Huber brothers, who also created ornaments for the Napoleon III apartments at the Château de Saint-Cloud, for the Paris Opera, and for the Council of State.*

TOP, FROM LEFT TO RIGHT *A guest's table setting in the Beauvais Room. Sky-painting by Nolau and Rubé. The room derives its name from the tapestries embroidered with birds by Charles Mangonot (1825–1900) lining the walls and above the doors woven at the end of the nineteenth century at the Beauvais Manufacture.*

ABOVE, FROM LEFT TO RIGHT *The overmantel. Limoges porcelain with the insignia of the Ministry for Foreign Affairs.*

FACING PAGE *On the first floor overhanging the garden, the Beauvais Room in a rotunda lends itself to work meetings and to the more exclusive receptions. The team of maîtres d' attends to their final instructions before beginning the service; they will have to synchronize their work in close collaboration with the chefs in the kitchen.*

FOLLOWING PAGES *The Grand Salon on the first floor, on the Seine side. To either side of the massive overmantel carved by Michel Joseph Napoleon Liénard hang portraits by the German painter Franz Xaver Winterhalter (1805–1873) showing the second daughter of Louis-Philippe, Marie d'Orléans, duchess of Württemberg (on the right), and Marie-Caroline de Bourbon, princess of Salerno and duchess of Aumale, the king's daughter-in-law (on the left).*

FACING PAGE *On the first floor, the antechamber looking over the Seine. In the foreground a Sèvres china vase from the nineteenth century; on the wall, The Port of Rochefort, a grisaille by John Quirin Jahn and Christophe Seckel, dating from the end of the eighteenth century.*

TOP, FROM LEFT TO RIGHT *The Port of Marseilles, late eighteenth-century grisaille by John Quirin Jahn and Christophe Seckel. The enfilade along the Seine seen from the anteroom. In the east hall, a Sèvres cup and saucer.*

BELOW, FROM LEFT TO RIGHT *Detail of a grisaille. Partial view of the second salon and a detail of one of its wall hangings.*

FOLLOWING PAGES *To the garden side, the so-called "King" bathroom that may be visited on open days during the Journées du Patrimoine. It was restored in 1938 for the visit of George VI by mosaicist and glassmaker Auguste Labouret (1871–1964) and decorator Jacques Adnet (1901–1984), who employed materials used at that time on luxury steamers: enamel, black marble with copper inclusions, chromium-plating, and glass mosaic. The glass wall was treated with sand and engraved.*

PAGES 26 AND 27 *The French-style garden along the south front extends as far as rue de l'Université. It is here that, on National Day, the minister receives his whole staff.*

HÔTEL DE BESENVAL

RESIDENCE OF THE AMBASSADOR
OF THE SWISS CONFEDERATION

HÔTEL DE BESENVAL

RESIDENCE OF THE AMBASSADOR OF THE SWISS CONFEDERATION

Date of construction 1705

Architect Pierre Alexis Delamair

WHEN, IN 1767, THE SWISS BARON, PIERRE-VICTOR DE BESENVAL, BOUGHT THE Hôtel Chanac de Pompadour on rue de Grenelle he could never have suspected that his new residence would one day become the embassy of his native land.

Lieutenant-general in the army of the king of France, inspector-general of the Swiss Guards, Besenval had been born in 1721 into a family of Swiss nobles who possessed an estate at Waldegg, near Soleure. This tireless collector of works of art and women purchased the residence as a pleasure dome.

The building had been erected in 1704 for a sober man of the Church, Abbé Pierre Chanac de Pompadour, and had later been occupied by a bishop of Rennes, Guérapin de Vauréal, who had also served as French ambassador to Spain.

It was a splendid single-floor residence, comprising a wing between courtyard and garden designed by Pierre Alexis Delamair, an architect who also built the Hôtel de Soubise and the Hôtel de Rohan in Paris. To Besenval's eyes, however, the construction seemed far too modest an affair, so he brought in the architect Brongniart and the sculptor Clodion to decorate certain rooms and to arrange a nymphaeum (one would now call it a "spa") in the basement. This room soon became famous in Paris for its suggestive decoration, with a languorous *Source* carved by Clodion and bas-reliefs representing *Venus and Love with Leda and the Swan* and *Pan pursuing Syrinx while Love Looks on*, today in the Louvre. Besenval would lounge about there with his conquests, such as the most faithful, the inimitable Marquise de La Suze, or else the Marquise Anne-Madeleine-Louise de Ségur, wife of the future Marshal of France, who even gave him a son, the Vicomte de Ségur.

Besenval's love life and military exploits would provide enough material for a multi-volume biography, so let us confine ourselves to mentioning that, on July 14, 1789, when the commander of the Swiss Guard did not have long to live, he refused to open fire on the mob that stormed the Bastille so as to avoid a bloodbath. Although his decision was supported by the King, he was accused of high treason, imprisoned for some time, judged, and finally exonerated. He died just two years later, bequeathing his gorgeous love-nest to the Maréchal de Ségur, knowing that it would thus be inherited by his illegitimate son, the Vicomte de Ségur.

The residence latterly fell into the hands of many different owners. In 1862, while being let to the Montholon de Semonville family by descendants of Lucien Bonaparte, a floor and an attic were added. Then it belonged to a Swiss national, Mme Baumann, before being acquired in 1938 by the Confederation. After serious restoration work, and the addition of an administrative building bordering the west court, the offices of the Swiss embassy opened in January 1939.

Visitors today can gaze in wonder at the ceremonial rooms. Splendid wood paneling greets them in the hall, a prelude to the eighteenth-century carvings that abound throughout the entire ground floor. Having passed through the Salon des Perroquets, which owes its name to the iridescent parrots perched in the overdoors—and having admired the grisailles on other overdoors in the Hall of the Ministers, one enters a charming little boudoir that is surely the most exquisite room in the whole building, with an alcove sheltering a sofa and four panels with medallions painted with the manner of Boucher framing four small vitrines.

PAGE 28 *With its plain paneling and hard limestone flags, the main hall is eminently characteristic of seventeenth-century classicism.*

PRECEDING PAGES *To either side of the door opening onto the Salon des Perroquets: on the right, Louis Pfyffer d'Altishofen of Lucerne, who entered French service in 1557 to defend King Charles IX against attack by Protestant forces; on the left, Georg Jenatsch, an ally of the Duc de Rohan during the Thirty Years War.*

FACING PAGE *Garden side. A small boudoir, known as the Salon de l'Alcôve, is lined with rare, eighteenth-century style carved wood paneling, and presents, in addition to a porcelain collection from the Nyon manufacture founded in Switzerland in 1781 and lent by the Nyon Museum of History and Porcelain, four medallions painted in the manner of François Boucher.*

Like a picture within a picture, above the sofa stands a canvas by Jules Didier (1831–1892) representing the Montholons in a rococo cabinet. To the opposite side, the Hall of Parrots opens on to a tapestry room graced with a monumental Gobelin hanging after cartoons by Le Brun representing the renewal of the alliance between Louis XIV and the ambassadors of the thirteen Swiss cantons in the cathedral of Notre Dame de Paris on November 18, 1663.

Several times a week, functions—breakfasts, lunches, and dinners—are given at the embassy. The dining room then becomes the beating heart of the residence: its spare neoclassical decor, created by Alexandre Théodore Brongniart (1739–1813), architect of Paris's famous stock exchange, has not changed since the time of Besenval—apart from a few more modern pictures, such as a splendid still-life by Vallotton. Here the overdoors are in stucco and depict antique mythological themes—*Dance of the Bacchantes*, *Toilet of Venus*—entirely in keeping with taste of that insatiable aesthete, the baron.

Some of the twenty-two guests seated at the ambassador's table may well take a liking to them, but they should not allow themselves to be distracted from the delights prepared by a French chef who has not only familiarized himself with Swiss specialties, such as Zurich-style émincé of veal, but also mastered a vast gamut of international cuisine, all accompanied by Swiss wines.

In addition to these meals, the ambassador's home plays host to various cultural events, including concerts and exhibitions. For it should not be forgotten that Switzerland has many friends in France and that no fewer than one hundred and seventy thousand of her nationals reside in the host country. ❧

Diner du mercredi 23 septembre 2009

Mousse de bar à la provençale
**

Risotto et paupiettes de veau à la tessinoise
**

Pêches aux amaretti

Coup de l'Étrier, Epesses 2008
Syrah du Valais, Vétroz 2007

TOP FROM LEFT TO RIGHT *Partial view of the dining room.*
A menu card engraved with the official emblem of
the Swiss Confederation. Detail of the table setting
ABOVE FROM LEFT TO RIGHT *A selection of the delicious*
dishes served by the French chef.
FACING PAGE *The table laid for a private dinner in the pastel*
green dining room designed in the neoclassical style
by Alexandre Théodore Brongniart (1739–1813).
Baron de Besenval also asked him to build a "bathing
temple" in the basement that has since disappeared,
though the bas-reliefs carved by Michel Clodion
(1738–1814) are presently in the Louvre.

FACING PAGE *On the ground floor, the Tapestry Room, a centrally placed reception space that houses a large hanging from the Gobelins manufacture celebrating the renewal of the alliance between the king of France, Louis XIV, and ambassadors from the thirteen Swiss cantons in the Cathedral of Notre-Dame in 1663. In the foreground, a rare Louis XVI furniture ensemble with themes from La Fontaine's Fables frames a fireplace dating from the beginning of the eighteenth century.*

TOP LEFT *In the Tapestry Room: portrait of Baron Pierre Victor de Besenval when inspector-general of the Swiss Guards in France in the reign of Louis XV.*
TOP MIDDLE *Partial view of the Ministers' Room contiguous to the small boudoir and the Hall of Parrots.*
TOP RIGHT *Detail of the Tapestry Room: needlepoint on one of the eighteenth-century chairs.*
ABOVE LEFT *Detail of the central scene of the tapestry woven in 1665 by the Gobelins manufacture after cartoons by Charles Le Brun.*
ABOVE RIGHT *A late nineteenth-century portable liquor chest with mother-of-pearl inlay.*

FACING PAGE *The bust of Diana in the park
has remained in place for more than three
hundred years.*
ABOVE LEFT *The north front giving on the garden.
The residence was surmounted by
an additional floor in the nineteenth century.*
ABOVE RIGHT *A bust of Flora.*
RIGHT *Detail of the English-style garden
commissioned by Baron de Besenval.*

HÔTEL
D'ESTRÉES

·

RESIDENCE OF THE AMBASSADOR
OF THE RUSSIAN FEDERATION

HÔTEL D'ESTRÉES

RESIDENCE OF THE AMBASSADOR OF THE RUSSIAN FEDERATION

Date of construction 1711–13

Architect Robert de Cotte

IN 1863, BARON DE BOUDBERG, RUSSIAN AMBASSADOR TO FRANCE, EXERCISED BY the exorbitant rents he had to pay for a residence in Paris, decided to buy a house in the name of the Russian State. His choice fell upon the Hôtel d'Estrées, which had been mortgaged by its owner, the Duc des Cars.

The mansion had been built between 1711 and 1713 by Robert de Cotte, "First Architect to the King" of Louis XIV, for Madeleine-Diane de Bautru de Vaubrun, widow of the Duc d'Estrées, *pair de France*. The duchess having no direct heir, the residence fell to her nephew, the Duc de Biron, who sold it on a year later to the Duchess of Modena, Charlotte-Aglaé d'Orléans, third daughter of the French Regent. By 1761, the building had been acquired by the Marquis de Beuvron d'Harcourt, *commissaire général* to the cavalry. Preserved by the Harcourt family until the Revolution, it had then been confiscated. The Empire had affected it to General Clarke, Duc de Feltre and Minister for War, before it was bought in 1823 by the Marquise de Tourzel, who then passed it to her daughter Augustine, wife of the aforementioned Duc des Cars.

The purchase of the residence by the Russian State thus brought a checkered history to an end. Even the Bolshevik Revolution failed to change much . . . if one excludes a portrait of Lenin in one room—as testified by a photograph of 1922—and the modest three-room apartment arranged on the ground floor for the ambassadors of the Communist era until the 1960s, which one can still see today. The residence's Communist interlude was curtailed, however, by the German Occupation, during which it was requisitioned and turned into offices for the Gestapo.

In 1977, all the diplomatic offices and consular services were transferred to the vast modern embassy that opened on boulevard Lannes, close to the Bois de Boulogne. Now solely serving as the ambassador's residence, intended both to house his family and to receive his many guests, the building was restored from top to bottom in 1978–80 by specialists from the State Hermitage Museum in the Second Empire style, already predominant in earlier redecorations.

Once through the imposing portal on rue de Grenelle and across the paved central courtyard, one climbs the steps of the marchioness's porticoed entrance (extremely rare in Paris). In the great monumental staircase visitors discover the most prestigious work of art of which the residence can boast: a vast Flemish tapestry from the beginning of the seventeenth century representing the deeds of Alexander the Great. The stairway leads up to the ceremonial rooms where major functions are held. The Salle Rouge—the Red Hall—furnished, like almost all the others, in a Louis XV style, is often the venue for musical soirées. Its overdoors painted by the school of Nicolas Lancret (1690–1743) represent mythological or gallant scenes; the wainscoting, doors, and ceilings are decorated and gilded in a Louis XV or Louis XVI style, but actually date from the Second Empire. This room then flows onto the current dining room, a charming blue oval, which served as Tsar Nicolas II's study when he stayed in Paris in 1896. In the lavish gilded decoration on the wall, the Soviet regime spared the "AA" monograms of Alexander III, the Imperial Russian coat of arms of the double-headed eagle, and a medallion of St. George slaying the dragon.

It is here that meals prepared by the Muscovite chef of the residence are served to the ambassador's guests on a blue-and-gold porcelain service made by the St. Petersburg Manufacture. The table can be laid for up to sixteen. Working lunches are served almost daily. Official buffet dinners, held on the occasion of cultural or political events, can number some two hundred guests.

The Red Hall gives onto the Gold Room, the residence's most sumptuous, which owes its name to its glorious gilt interior, comprising four grooved columns with Corinthian capitals and overdoors decorated with scenes drawn from the *Fables* of La Fontaine. Finally there comes the Green Room, formerly the dining room of the ambassador of Imperial Russia. Painted in pale green, the walls are hung with five paintings of an Italianate Flemish stamp and a canvas by Ivan Ayvazovsky (1817–1900), a major Russian painter of Armenian extraction, celebrated for his seascapes. *Mirage* shows a highly romanticized Constantinople seen from the sea through the fog.

The residence also houses official apartments for the Head of the State and the government, the Foreign Minister, and other Russian personages when they come to the French capital, as well as those of the ambassador and his personnel.

These private apartments are not shown to the six thousand or so people who visit the Hôtel d'Estrées during the Journées du Patrimoine when many official buildings are open to the public in France, though, in addition to the ceremonial rooms, they are more than welcome to enjoy the charm of the lush French-style gardens. ❧

Salade à la russe

◆

Borchtch à la Moscovite

◆

Côtelettes « Pojarsky »

◆

Sorbet de crème brûlée aux fruits frais

◆

Thé, café

TOP LEFT *Detail of the Gold Room: gilt-bronze plaque on an inlaid wood pedestal in the Boulle manner.*
TOP CENTER *A menu card emblazoned with the national emblem of the Russian Federation.*
TOP RIGHT *Detail of the Gold Room: a porcelain and bronze vase.*
ABOVE LEFT *Arches and cornices in the Gold Room.*
ABOVE CENTER *The residence's official "cobalt net"-pattern dinner service, a replica of an original made for Empress Catherine II.*
ABOVE RIGHT *A menu as served at the residence.*
FACING PAGE *The dining table in the Gold Room.*

ABOVE *The antechamber in the eighteenth-century style opens onto the Gold Room.*
FACING PAGE *A decorative bronze surtout stands on a rococo console in the Gold Room.*
PAGE 54 *Detail of the Green Room: one of the gold-painted Empire-style amphora vases.*

PAGE 55 *First floor, garden side. During the Russian Empire the Green Room served as an official dining hall. At the present time, the head of State, the head of the Government, and his ministers all dine here when visiting officially.*

PAGE 56 *A small oval salon with the monograms "A.A."*
referring to Emperor Alexander III serves today
as the everyday dining-room.
PAGE 57 *The Red Room—known in the tsarist era*
as the Throne Room—is now a venue for musical
soirées. The gallant scenes on the overdoors dating
from the construction of the residence are attributed
to the school of Nicolas Lancret (1690–1743).
ABOVE *The south front of the residence giving on*
to the garden. In the nineteenth century, the building
was extended by a further storey with a balustrade
running round the entire roof.
FACING PAGE *The central stairway leading to the garden*
à la française *that stretches as far as the rue*
de Varenne.

HÔTEL DE
BEAUHARNAIS

·

RESIDENCE OF THE AMBASSADOR
OF THE FEDERAL REPUBLIC OF GERMANY

HÔTEL DE BEAUHARNAIS

RESIDENCE OF THE AMBASSADOR OF THE FEDERAL REPUBLIC OF GERMANY

Date of construction 1713–15

Architect Germain Boffrand

THE GERMAN AMBASSADOR TO FRANCE RESIDES IN A HOUSE WHICH OWES EVERY-thing to Eugène de Beauharnais, who was counseled by Joséphine, his mother, first wife of Napoleon I and empress of France from 1804 to 1809. Frozen in time, this splendid Faubourg Saint-Germain residence on the banks of the Seine is a prime example—unique in the world because it remains totally intact—of the decorative pomp and circumstance of the First Empire. Joséphine's son, Eugène—adopted by Bonaparte—had acquired it on May 20, 1803. As an officer constantly on campaign, and soon summoned to take up his viceroyalty in Italy, he entrusted the task of decorating and altering it into the hands of his mother, aided by an architect and a steward. She was elegant and refined, but also madly extravagant: the building thus became one of the most luxurious residences in all Paris. Work started during summer 1804, just after she had been proclaimed empress and her son Italian viceroy.

The building on the rue de Lille (at the "rue de Bourbon") had been erected by the architect Germain Boffrand in 1713–15 and immediately sold to Marquis Jean-Baptiste Colbert de Torcy, nephew of Louis XIV's celebrated minister. It had subsequently belonged to the Duc de Villeroy, governor of Lyon, then, after he was executed during the Revolution, passed to a certain Pierre Joseph Garnier, who originally rented it to Eugène before finally letting him buy it. Eugène, detained in Italy or busy on the battle-field, in fact almost never lived here. Refitted and redecorated entirely by Joséphine, from 1809 it was used to house Napoleon's guests to Paris.

PAGE 60 *The main entrance is preceded by a portico "à l'égyptienne" in honor of Napoleon's campaigns in Egypt in 1798. Erected in 1804 by the architect appointed by Josephine de Beauharnais, the portico is a rare example of this Egyptian-style architecture in Paris.*
RIGHT *Detail of the Salon Rouge on the first floor: Prince Eugène de Beauharnais (Josephine's son)—in exile after the fall of the Empire—painted by Joseph Karl Stieler (1781–1858).*
FACING PAGE *View through the double doors from the main vestibule.*

In 1814, after the fall of the Empire, Eugène took refuge with his father-in-law, King Max-Joseph of Bavaria (whose daughter, Augusta Amelia, he had married in 1805), and afterwards let the residence complete with its treasures and furniture to King Frederick William III of Prussia, who turned it into the headquarters of his Paris legation. The king was to purchase it two years later, making it the residence of the Prussian ambassadors, the most famous, Bismarck, residing here in 1862. The building has been somewhat altered over the course of time. Closed up during the First World War, but with its extraterritoriality respected, the residence was confiscated after the Second World War, being allocated to various branches of the administration. Although listed as an historic building in 1951, it was in rather poor shape when it was returned to the Federal Republic ten years later.

General de Gaulle requested that the German authorities restore it. The whole process cost some twenty million marks, but at length the Hôtel de Beauharnais reemerged in its original Empire glory, together with all its valuable furniture and objects. So it is that guests of the ambassador today—once through a portico that reproduces the entryway to an ancient Egyptian temple and across the accesses to the main courtyard—discover Eugène's residence just as he designed it, down to the tiniest detail.

The portico represents the first of many "Egyptian" references here, reflections of a French passion that had been recently kindled by Napoleon's expedition to the Nile. The most delicious is certainly the "Turkish-style" boudoir on the first floor, a relatively faithful replica, in miniature, of a room in an Oriental palace, complete with a painted and carved wood arcade decor and an extraordinary ornamental frieze depicting scenes from the harem and slave market. The original Versailles parquet floor also survives. Orientalism resurfaces in the Salon des Mamelouks on the ground floor, decorated with portraits of Mamluks, the ruling military cast in Ottoman Egypt dating from the Egyptian campaign. The space today serves as a small dining room.

One should also mention the large pink granite obelisk decorating the fireplace in the larger dining room, a very rare clock with Arabic figures in the Throne Room, and a set of vases and candlesticks with Egyptian slave motifs signed Pierre-Philippe Thomire (the creator of a great number of valuable bronzes still in the residence) in the Salon des Quatre Saisons.

The many wonders one glimpses as one crosses the library, the Salon Vert, or the Salon des Quatre Saisons distributed over the first two floors of the residence and used for receptions include furniture by the great cabinetmaker Jacob-Desmalter, paintings by Hubert Robert (1723–1808), and panels attributed to Louis Girodet-Trioson (1767–1824).

In addition to the boudoir *à la turque*, other rooms attract particular attention: the bedroom of Hortense de Beauharnais whose majestic four-poster has bronze-decorated columns, a piece by Jacob-Desmalter; the adjacent bathroom, still intact, with its mirrored walls, zinc bathtub, decor of colonnettes, and polychrome marble flooring depicting Europe on the bull; all painted wood, the Music Room represents the Muses. Its armchairs are decorated with swans (once again by Jacob) with a recurrent lute motif; while in the recently restored Salon Cerise, which owes its name to the color of the lampas covering its walls, a spectacular mantelpiece adorned with wild animals, birds, and butterflies in micro-mosaic can be admired.

The Hôtel de Beauharnais is however not simply an attractive encyclopedia of the Empire style; it is also a diplomatic residence of a major European power catering for thousands of French and Germans every year.

October 3, the date of German Reunification, sees a garden party for nearly two thousand guests who savor specialties from a given Land, a different one each year. The reception is held in the vast garden overlooking the Seine. Three or four times a year, concerts are given in the large dining room for an audience of a hundred: a Lieder piano recital or chamber music presents an opportunity to discover young German talents. The traditional savory German breakfast, the *Frühstück*, means the ambassador can start his working day in the company of his collaborators or some other important figure. The diplomat is also fond of private working lunches around a small table laid in the Salon des Mamelouks.

And last but not least, he may be joined by up to thirty personalities from the worlds of politics, economics, or culture in frequent dinner debates.

It is on these occasions that the recently appointed German head cook to the residence, who has worked under Antoine Westermann and other world-renowned chefs, can give free rein to his talents in the shape of a traditional German cuisine given a radically up-to-date twist. On a table that the ambassadress likes to swathe in plentiful flowers, dishes are served on a "Kurland" porcelain service in production at the prestigious Berlin manufactory of K.P.M. (the Königliche Porzellan Manufaktur) since 1790. ❖

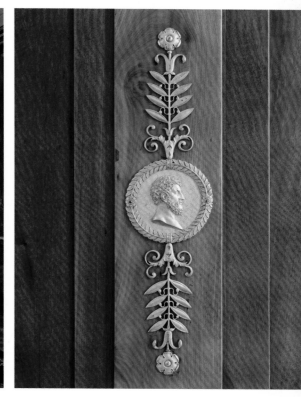

ABOVE LEFT *Detail of the table setting: the porcelain figurines, made by the Nymphenburg manufacture, are composed into a centerpiece.*

ABOVE RIGHT *Detail of the Kurland porcelain service employed at the residence and made since the eighteenth century at the KPM manufacture in Berlin.*

LEFT *Detail of the small dining room. The portrait of one of the sheikhs who agreed to negociate with Napoleon Bonaparte during his Egyptian campaign.*

FACING PAGE *The table is usually laid in the small dining room known as the "Salon des Mamelouks" because of the paintings by Michel Rigo, who produced a similar series for Malmaison.*

LEFT *The Salon des Quatre Saisons. Detail of the so-called "Emperor" table top, embellished with a portrait in porcelain made by the Clignancourt manufacture.*
BELOW *General view of the Salon des Quatre Saisons looking over the garden.*
FACING PAGE *View of part of the Salon des Quatre Saisons dedicated to the decorative arts from the First Empire. The female figures on the walls personify the seasons and are ascribed to the studio of Louis Girodet-Trioson (1767–1824). In the center stands the drum-shaped "Emperor" table presented to Prince Eugène by the City of Paris.*
PAGE 72 *Detail of the Salon des Quatre Saisons: a vase with a centaur motif in chased copper and gilt bronze, cast by the bronze-founder Claude Galle (1759–1815).*
PAGE 73 *Detail of the Salon des Quatre Saisons: under the frieze with eagles refurbished in the nineteenth century by Jacques Ignace Hittorff (1792–1867) and framed by sconces by bronze-founder Pierre-Philippe Thomire (1751–1843), an allegory of Winter attributed to the studio of Louis Girodet-Trioson.*

ABOVE *Details of the Salon des Quatre Saisons: figurines painted on a door leaf and a gallery of gilt-bronze brackets on a console table.*
FACING PAGE *Detail of the Salon des Quatre Saisons: a partial view of the stucco and papier-mâché ceiling added in the nineteenth century by the architect Jacques Ignace Hittorff (1792–1867), illumined by motifs characteristic of the First Empire such as palmettes, whorls, eagles, and vine-fronds.*

LEFT *Glimpse of the Music Room from the hall of the first floor.*
BELOW LEFT *Detail of the Music Room: a painted frieze of putti runs along the cornice.*
BELOW RIGHT *Detail of the Music Room: a frieze painted with swans borders each fresco.*
FACING PAGE *View of part of the Music Room with frescoes painted in the time of Eugène and furnished with chairs with decorative arms in the shape of swans. The composer Richard Wagner (1813–1883) stayed in the residence at the time of a performance of Tannhäuser in Paris.*
FOLLOWING DOUBLE PAGES *The Turkish boudoir adjoining the bathroom was somewhere one could rest after the bath. Inspired by the Ottoman style, its furniture, painted decor, and Versailles-style parquet flooring survive intact.*

FACING PAGE *The garden side. General view of the Salon Cerise, whose name derives from the cherry color of the lampas lining the walls. At the windows, the silks and the netting are draped in the Empire manner. This cerise-colored room, refurbished with original furniture as noted in Eugène's inventory drawn up in 1817, was restored from floor to ceiling in 2009.*
RIGHT *View of part of the Salon Cerise.*
BELOW LEFT *Details of the Salon Cerise: two motifs on the mantelpiece in micro-mosaic by Francesco Belloni (1772–1863).*
BELOW RIGHT *Detail of the Salon Cerise: tiebacks on a window giving on the garden.*

LEFT *Detail of the bedroom named after Prince Eugène's sister, Hortense: the chandelier and the only original painted ceiling.*
BELOW LEFT *Hortense's bedchamber: detail of bronzes ornamenting the sleigh bed.*
BELOW RIGHT *Hortense's bedroom: detail of a painting on silk under glass and applied to one of the commode's panels.*
FACING PAGE *Queen Hortense's chamber with the four poster in light mahogany attributed to François Honoré Jacob-Desmalter. The silk hangings were restored using information from the Prelle manufacture archives in Lyon.*
FOLLOWING DOUBLE PAGES *North front of the Hôtel Beauharnais. The garden planted, as Eugène de Beauharnais wished, in the English manner, extends to the quai de la Seine. On the national holiday, it can cater for over than one thousand guests.*

HÔTEL
D'AVARAY

RESIDENCE OF THE AMBASSADOR
OF THE KINGDOM OF THE NETHERLANDS

The ambassadorial residence is thus an accessible place where the em
the exchange of ideas and projects under the umbrella of the Franco-Dutch
Council, set up in 2003.

Several times a month, the ambassador also receives politicians, busine
personalities from every walk of life for a lunch or dinner at which guests of
alities swap points of view through interpreters. The dining-room table has
up to twenty-four guests, though when that number is exceeded small rour
ten can be laid in the Music Room. It is here too that dinner-concerts are hel
ber music generally—organized in co-operation with the Netherlands Institu

The ambassador takes a special interest in the composition of the menu i
with the Italian chef of the residence, a fine vegetarian cook who is also a
French and Asian cuisine, as well as his own.

On two occasions a year, the host outdoes himself: April 29 sees the "Tu
organized for French associates, while the following day is "Queen's Day,"
cally celebrated by the Dutch contingent. These two events are attended by
people, against a marvelous floral backdrop, the food served at the buffe
"homemade" by the chef and his assistant cooks.

The guests meanwhile can take the opportunity of discovering this elegan
standing at 85 rue de Grenelle and built between 1720 and 1723 by the arc
Baptiste Leroux for Claude-Théophile de Bésiade, Marquis d'Avaray. An em
mat who filled posts in Switzerland and in Flanders, the client had no time
residence and so rented it to Horatio Walpole, then British ambassador.

The d'Avarays kept the building in the family until 1920, the year that sa
sition by the Dutch government. John Loudon, ambassador between the
undertook to overhaul it thoroughly, restoring it to its long-lost eighteenth-ce
He also added the period wood-paneling in a rather sober style that gives a s
tonality to the reception space and installed a splendid dining room in the we
formerly housed the stables.

Finally, all the rooms were bedecked in pictures, objets d'art, and furniture lent by the Dutch government. The Loudon family itself presented several works from its personal collections, including the sumptuous three-part Aubusson tapestry that adorns the dining room. The architectural and artistic treasures of the building would fill a small volume. One first notices from the vestibule the majestic main staircase, bordered by double wrought-iron banisters of Louis XV style. Traversing the whole space, the library, set between the main courtyard and the garden, is the preferred place for informal receptions, whether a work meeting or some larger scale function.

Fine pictures from the Mauritshuis in The Hague or from the Rijksmuseum in Amsterdam grace the Louis XIV paneling. As for the great hall, decorated with glorious sixteenth-century Brussels tapestries teeming with animals, it hosts much-anticipated annual festivities such as the Tulip Festival.

The dining room, whose imposing trompe l'oeil tapestry of undergrowth and gardens has already been referred to, is also decorated with two large seventeenth-century paintings, two *japonisant* commodes that recall The Netherlands' long history of trading with the Land of the Rising Sun, and one charming cabinet displaying a shell motif in inlaid wood evoking the Netherlands' rich history in exotic lands.

The upper floor houses the ambassador's apartments that look out on the residence's most illustrious feature: the splendid garden *à la française* with its three extensive flowerbeds. In spring, he might also care to admire—as the ambassador put it himself—a "field of Dutch tulips composed in the French style": a garden that symbolizes an ancient and enduring amity. ❧

Detail of the great room: a "still-life" featuring an eighteenth-century silver teapot with ivory handle.
Partial view of the great room with Regency-period wood paneling dedicated to the art of music and with overdoors showing pastoral scenes ascribed to François Boucher (1703–1770), remounted in situ. Today, this hall, opening on to the garden, serves various purposes: concerts, seminars, conferences, and work meetings.

Déjeuner en l'honneur
des membres du Conseil de
Coopération franco-néerlandais

* * * * * *

Buisson d'asperge aux anguilles

* * *

Trilogie néerlandaise au caviar de hareng

* * *

Aumônière aux fruits rouges

* * *

Pouilly Fumé   2006
Tonelum

FACING PAGE

TOP LEFT *The chef at work in the pantry
giving on the court.*

TOP RIGHT *Armorial device of the Kingdom
of the Netherlands engraved on crystal glass.*

BOTTOM LEFT *The "buisson aux anguilles"
prepared by the residence's chef.*

BOTTOM RIGHT *An official menu card featuring
the lion of Nassau and the national motto,
"Je maintiendrai."*

RIGHT *Detail of the dining room:
an eighteenth-century silver coffee urn
decorated with an ivory palmette.*

BELOW *In the main hall, a collection
of nineteenth-century Delft porcelain vases,
surmounted by Chinese dogs of Fo.*

FACING PAGE *Decorated in the French Regency style, the dining room giving onto the court was created at the beginning of the twentieth century in the west wing on the site of the stables. The room is employed for official dinners as well as for working breakfasts.*

ABOVE *View of the garden from the library lined with unpainted carved paneling from the Louis XIV era. The room houses any number of masterpieces of seventeenth-century Dutch painting, including a naval engagement by Willem Van de Velde the Younger (1633–1707) and a skirmish between horsemen by Jan Van Huchtenburgh (1647–1733), a painter much appreciated by William III of Orange.*

FACING PAGE *General view of the garden planted in the French style.*

RIGHT *The south front skirting the garden, with the pediment surmounted by the coat of arms of the residence's first owners, the Bésiade d'Avaray family.*

BELOW LEFT *A bed of tulips. Just some of the ten thousand bulbs specially planted for the annual Tulip Festival, a festival that attracts nearly nine hundred guests. A similar number come for Queen's Day.*

BELOW RIGHT *An armillary sphere (astronomical instrument) dating from the eighteenth century; one of only three surviving specimens in Paris.*

HÔTEL
DE CHAROST

·

RESIDENCE OF THE AMBASSADOR
OF THE UNITED KINGDOM OF GREAT BRITAIN
AND NORTHERN IRELAND

HÔTEL DE CHAROST

RESIDENCE OF THE AMBASSADOR OF THE UNITED KINGDOM OF GREAT BRITAIN AND NORTHERN IRELAND

Date of construction 1722–25

Architect Antoine Mazin

SAVE PERHAPS FOR THE CHANNEL TUNNEL, THERE CAN BE FEWER MORE TELLING symbols of Franco-British friendship—ratified diplomatically more than a century ago with the Entente Cordiale—than the Paris residence of the ambassador of the United Kingdom, where the furniture used by Her Majesty's representative once belonged to Napoleon's favorite sister, Pauline Borghese.

Pauline settled in this vast mansion in the Faubourg Saint-Honoré in August 1803, a few weeks prior to her marriage to the Roman prince, Camillo Borghese. At this date, it still belonged to the Charost family, who had hitherto rented it to the British ambassador Lord Whitworth, abruptly recalled to London shortly before the declaration of war between the two countries on May 18. Pauline signed her wedding agreement there on August 23 and bought it from the Duchesse de Charost on November 3.

This fine, classical building was erected in 1722 by the architect Antoine Mazin on behalf of a duke and lieutenant-general in the king's army, Paul-François de Béthune-Charost. It was occupied by the Charost family until 1784 when it was rented to Auguste d'Arenberg, Comte de La Marck, a scion at once French and Austrian who had attempted to save the royal family after the Revolution. He left France definitively for Austria in 1792. The Duc de Charost, owner of the residence during this period of upheaval, was arrested but escaped the Terror by the skin of his teeth. He recovered all his property, even becoming mayor of the tenth arrondissement (today, the seventh arrondissement) in 1799.

The building, however, had been stripped of all its furniture and stood empty by the time his widow rented it to Lord Whitworth, the ambassador moving in with his own furniture (which he later took with him when he departed his post). Thus, when Pauline Borghese installed her household and later acquired the residence, she had to have furniture brought in quickly from her former homes. Over the years, she furnished it with splendid Empire pieces, as well as with various decorative objects, including a great number of candelabra and clocks that remain *in situ* today.

PAGE 100 *The court front is embellished with the kind of pediment and antique peristyle much in vogue in the eighteenth century.*
RIGHT *Detail of the grand entrance hall. Pauline Bonaparte Borghese (1780–1825) poses as Venus Victrix for the sculptor Antonio Canova (1757–1822); the original is in the Galleria Borghese in Rome. In the background stands the bust of George Villiers, 5th Earl of Jersey.*
FACING PAGE *The grand hall graced with six Ionic columns has survived unchanged through the years. In front of the entrance stands a portrait of Queen Victoria at the beginning of her reign, a copy of the original by Franz Xaver Winterhalter (1805–1873), Her Majesty's favorite painter. The main staircase leads up to the less formal reception rooms on the upper floor.*

FACING PAGE *An eighteenth-century gilt-iron banister rail by master ironworker Antoine Hallé sweeps round the great staircase.*
BELOW LEFT *Detail of the main hall: a white marble bust of the First Duke of Wellington next to another of Napoleon.*
BELOW RIGHT *Detail of the gilt-iron motifs on the banister rail on the grand staircase.*

In addition to the furniture, the main transformation ordained by Pauline was the addition of two extensive wings to the garden side, one to show her husband's art collection, the other to serve as large dining room with space for about sixty diners. It also seems that she had the great hall partitioned off, partly for reasons of security. Having become imperial princess in 1804, and in the habit of receiving guests and lovers, sometimes even hushing up the emperor's extramarital affairs, Pauline had to be well protected. Lastly, the princess undertook to replace the outmoded wood-paneling, having the walls lined with precious cloths, complete with matching draw-curtains and seat-covers.

After the emperor's first abdication in 1814, Pauline decided to follow him to the island of Elba and thus had to sell off her home, by then one of the most lavish in Paris, together with all its furniture.

The British government could thus acquire the lot at a knockdown price, converting it into a residence for its ambassador, the Duke of Wellington. More than thirty representatives have since succeeded the Duke in occupying its matchless interior. Only a few adjustments have been made, such as refitting both garden wings (the art gallery has been converted into a ballroom) and constructing an arcade between them to plans executed by the architect Louis Visconti in 1825. From the great hall to the salons on the ground- and first floors, what visitors discover today is very much Pauline's palace. Only a few English pictures on the walls (lent by the Government Art Collection), typical British hospitality, and many of the events hosted by the ambassador betray its current function.

BELOW LEFT *Detail of the Salon Pauline: decoration on a gilded bronze candelabrum characteristic of the First Empire.*

BELOW CENTER *Detail of the Salon Pauline: one of the gilded bronze firedogs that once belonged to Pauline.*

BELOW RIGHT *Detail of the Salon Pauline: the room opens to the Salon Bleu by way of a glazed archway above the fireplace.*

FACING PAGE *The appearance of Pauline's private chamber as she would have seen it has been reconstructed in the Salon Pauline on the ground floor with the original Empire furniture described in the 1814 inventory; her bed surmounted by the imperial eagle was used by British ambassadors until 1982. The room was at one time called the Salon Victoria, in honor of the queen's sojourns in the residence.*

PAGE 108 *The Salon Rouge: a detail of the drops of a chandelier with twenty-four lights originally in Pauline's bedchamber.*

PAGE 109 *The Red Room lined with damask with the "Saint-Cloud palm" pattern today serves as a dining room for more informal receptions. To the left of the mirror, the portrait of Arthur Wellesley, First Duke of Wellington, the victor over Emperor Napoleon at the Battle of Waterloo in 1815. In the mirror is reflected the portrait of Lady Stuart de Rothesay, together with her two daughters, the wife of Charles Stuart, the British ambassador who succeeded the Duke of Wellington in 1815.*

Among the innumerable treasures scattered about the residence one should mention, on the ground floor, beneath the great Louis XV staircase, a reduced-size replica of the famous figure of Pauline in the attitude of Venus by Antonio Canova; in the Red Room, the "Minerva" clock in pinchbeck (a mock-gold alloy) by major sculptor and bronze-caster Pierre-Philippe Thomire (1751–1843), to whom is also owed the twenty-four stick chandelier in the same room; then, in the Blue Room, another clock, this time on the subject of "study staying the advance of time," where the hours are indicated by a revolving terrestrial sphere flanked by two symbolic figures in bronze; in the Pauline Room, the princess's own bed, the corners of the frame adorned with four Egyptian-style caryatids and surmounted by an oval tester in carved and gilded wood; in the Throne Room hangs a portrait of Queen Victoria aged nineteen by Sir George Hayter. Having ascended the majestic grand staircase, the visitor discovers, in the anteroom, a splendid full-sized portrait of Pauline in court dress by Robert Lefèvre (1755–1830); in the same room one can admire two pairs of candelabra representing Apollo and Aurora (Dawn) on gilded spheres; in the dining room, tapestries show intriguing scenes of everyday life in the seventeenth century; in the Cooper Bedroom, an extremely rare dressing-table by cabinetmaker François Joseph Loven, which once stood in the princess's bathroom.

Two final rooms testify to the impact on the intellectual and artistic spheres in postwar Paris of ambassador Duff Cooper and his very beautiful and brilliant wife, Lady Diana: the library created in 1944 in the former bedroom of Prince Borghese, the interior designed with the assistance of three celebrated decorators of the time: Charles de Beistegui, Georges Geoffroy, and Christian Bérard. This last also revamped the bathroom, where lengths of blue and white-striped canvas make it look like a Napoleonic War campaign tent.

A private museum then, certainly, but essentially this is a diplomatic residence that receives around fifteen thousand people a year, including three thousand for the open days of the Journées du Patrimoine, when the public is allowed to visit some of the city's private houses and monuments.

Daily, practically, the ambassador and his wife receive guests for breakfast, lunch, or dinner. The French chef, who has been at the ovens for nearly forty years, prepares a French cuisine together with the tastiest ingredients from the other side of the Channel: Scottish salmon, Hereford beef, and cheeses from Britain's rich farm lands.

The residence also plays host to a great many events of every kind: political, economic, or cultural, ranging from business seminars to catwalk shows. From spring on, guests can saunter round the marvelous garden—planted in the English manner, naturally—and boasting the finest lawn in the capital, extending as far as avenue Gabriel. ❖

**Ambassade de Grande-Bretagne, Paris
Dîner**

Trio de Saumon Ecossais
Scones à la Ciboulette

≈

Selle d'Agneau Pré-Salé Gallois
Sauce à la Gelée de Groseilles
Panais Rôtis
Purée de Pommes de Terre et Poireaux

≈

Salade
Fromages Fermiers Britanniques

≈

Glace à la Fleur de Sureau
Fruits Rouges Caramélisés

≈

*Chapel Down Bacchus 2005
Château Léoville-Barton 1995*

ABOVE *Detail of the Red Room: leaning against a magnificent
Empire candlestick, an official menu card inscribed
with the armorial bearings of the United Kingdom.*
FACING PAGE *Detail of the Red Room: for informal dinners
the ambassador's table is set directly on the mahogany top.
The Egyptian figure candelabra on the mantelpiece
frame a clock dedicated to Minerva, works by Empire
bronze-founder, Pierre-Philippe Thomire (1751–1843).*
FOLLOWING DOUBLE PAGES *West wing, garden front. The ballroom,
redecorated in the mid-nineteenth century by Etienne
Raveaux on the site of Pauline's picture gallery. The official
dinner given in 2004 on the occasion of a state visit
by Queen Elizabeth II was held here. Today the ballroom
is the venue for any number of cultural events.*

BELOW *An anteroom contiguous to the Duff Cooper Library. On the gueridon table, an equestrian statue of Edward VII, the son of Queen Victoria.*
FACING PAGE *On the first floor, to the court side, the library Ambassador Duff Cooper had installed on his arrival at the post in 1944, and which he enriched with books from his own collection. Nowadays the room serves as the present incumbent's private office.*

PRECEDING PAGES *On the garden side, first floor:*
tea is served in the Yellow Room, which owes
its name to the color of the lampas with
the "Four Continents" motif covering the walls.
The armchairs are part of the furniture Pauline
intended for the picture gallery occupying
the ground floor in the west wing. The architect
Louis Visconti converted the picture gallery
into what is today the ballroom.

ABOVE *The Blue Room giving through to the arcaded veranda features*
furnishings that belonged to Pauline, including a thirty-lamp chandelier
adorned with a cockerel-head motif. The floor is laid with a copy of
an Aubusson carpet from the nineteenth century with the monogram
of King Louis-Philippe from the collection of the family of
the dukes of Hamilton, Scotland.
FACING PAGE *The garden, seen from the veranda connecting the two wings*
built on the initiative of the architect Louis Visconti, which today houses
works by contemporary British artists lent by the Government Art Collection.

HÔTEL DE LA ROCHEFOUCAULD-DOUDEAUVILLE

·

RESIDENCE OF THE AMBASSADOR
OF THE ITALIAN REPUBLIC

HÔTEL DE LA ROCHEFOUCAULD-DOUDEAUVILLE

RESIDENCE OF THE AMBASSADOR OF THE ITALIAN REPUBLIC

Date of construction 1732–33
Architect Jean-Sylvain Cartaud

PAGE 122 *Clad in more than four different French marbles, the main staircase, erected in the nineteenth century by the architect Henri Parent at the demand of the Duc de Doudeauville, harks back to the Escalier de la Reine in the Château de Versailles. The marble sets off three tapestries woven in the eighteenth century at the Gobelins Manufacture after cartoons by Jean-François de Troy (1679–1752).*
BELOW LEFT *The court front of the residence, erected in the eighteenth century, disposes of two entryways, both located in the wings.*
BELOW RIGHT *Altered in the nineteenth century, the second entrance is decorated with a tapestry, the Departure of Jason and Medea after the Capture of the Golden Fleece, executed in the eighteenth century by the Gobelins Manufacture after models by Jean-François de Troy.*
FACING PAGE *A marble half-barrel vault before the main entrance: extending beneath the main staircase, this technical tour de force by the architect conceals two secret doors.*

IN 1909, THE FRENCH STATE ACQUIRED FROM THE ITALIAN GOVERNMENT THE PALAZZO Farnese in Rome that it had been renting as its embassy since 1874. As the palace is an historic artifact of immense significance, a rider in the contract allowed the possibility of Italy's buying it back after a period of twenty-five years. The allotted time having elapsed, in 1934 the State opted to exercise this right. After lengthy discussions complicated by the darkening international situation, the following year the two parties manage to thrash out an agreement: Italy regained ownership of the palace and would lease it to France—for the symbolic fee of one lira per annum—on a 99-year lease. In exchange, France would commit to renting to Italy, at a similar peppercorn rate, a mansion in the Faubourg Saint-Germain as the site of the Italian embassy. To this purpose, in 1937 France purchased the splendid Hôtel de Boisgelin (also known as the Hôtel de La Rochefoucauld-Doudeauville), located at 47 rue de Varenne, and presented it to the Italian State.

To allow comparison with the Farnese Palace, the building must be opulent indeed. It does not disappoint. Erected in 1732 and 1733, its ample, soberly elegant lines had been designed by an architect, Jean-Sylvain Cartaud, a sworn enemy of the rococo, working for a wealthy banker, Gérard Heusch de Janvry, who had purchased a position as secretary to the king. The diverse furnishings and decors that had accrued over the years had only made the palace more splendid.

After the death of de Janvry, the residence was occupied by Camille de Lorraine, Prince de Marsan, and then by the archbishop of Aix-en-Provence, Raymond de Boisgelin. Seized at the Revolution, it was sold in 1807 to the Comte Bigot de Préameneu, a former lawyer at the Parliament de Paris (that is, a constitutional court) appointed by Bonaparte to draft the *Code Civil*.

Thirty years later, a new owner surfaced: the Comte de Bourbon-Conti. After his death in 1840, his widow remarried with Louis-Sosthène de La Rochefoucauld, Duc de Doudeauville, himself a widow and already father of three children. The duke was director of the Beaux-Arts during the Restoration and a great lover of the arts. In 1876, his second son, Marie-Charles-Sosthène de La Rochefoucauld, Duc de Bisaccia, became owner of the residence he had occupied for seventeen years. Deputy for the Sarthe and monarchist, two years earlier he had served as ambassador to London. In about 1868, he undertook a vast program of enlarging and restoring the building directed by the architect Henri Parent. The spectacular entrance halls and the ceremonial staircase in polychrome marble date from this period. In 1937, the residence was sold by his children to an investment arm of the public

finances, the Caisse des Dépôts et Consignations, who then transferred it to the Italian State. A new campaign of works promptly began, including the installation of decorative elements taken from palaces in Italy, resulting in its splendidly lavish appearance today.

One of its highpoints is undoubtedly the great hall in which has been reinstated the interior from an eighteenth-century theater removed lock, stock, and barrel from a palace in Palermo, the Palazzo Butera. Now reconfigured by antique dealer and decorator Adolfo Loewi, a specialist in Italian art, the former theater has been reinstalled as the interior for a ballroom built by the French architect, Félix Brunau. The result of this collaboration between two talents is an extraordinary blend of historical elements—the wealth of eighteenth-century Neapolitan paneling—and a backdrop that sets them off to perfection, including mirror-glass doors, a ceiling embellished with an understated floral decor also inspired by a villa in Palermo, and the ornamental wood painted with scenes in an eighteenth-century manner.

Adolfo Loewi is also the brains behind a number of the residence's other wonders: the small library decorated with paintings by Cignaroli (1730–1800) and today graced by an eighteenth-century desk inlaid with some exquisite marquetry of art deco flavor in the 1930s; the Chinese Room with Venetian furniture, a mix of authentic Far Eastern details and four large contemporary panels inspired by historic chinoiseries depicting female figures; and the first-floor dining room, entirely devoted to displaying five large pictures by Gian Antonio Guardi.

In addition to this newly set up and undeniably "Italian" decor—to which should be added a great number of works of art lent by museums in the Peninsula—the residence also boasts a mass of gorgeous details dating from the time of the La Rochefoucauld-Doudeauville family: eighteenth-century wainscoting and overdoors representing children's games from the Château de Bercy, ascribed to Nicolas Bertin (situated in the Salle des Jeux d'enfants on the first floor) and eighteenth-century Gobelins tapestries after cartoons by Jean-François de Troy that adorn the stairhall and other rooms.

TOP LEFT TO RIGHT, TOP TO BOTTOM *The Sicilian theater: detail of the rocaille woodwork either side of the stage. A niche in a panel of Venetian mirror glass. Detail on the ceiling: a delicate plant motif in wrought iron by Adolfo Loewi. One of the motifs painted in distemper onto the wooden paneling. Detail on one of the remounted wooden panels.* FACING PAGE *View of the Sicilian theatre. The original decor was restored and augmented with rocaille ornaments made by artisans from Venice.*

Throughout the year, this dazzling backdrop plays host to a vast number of events—first and foremost, the reception held on the national holiday, June 2. If the weather is fine, hundreds of guests saunter about the beautiful garden planted in the English style and admire two large statues of Diana (after works by Coysevox and Frémin now in the Louvre). Conferences are frequently held in the Sicilian theater, as well as Italian product presentations, fashion parades, and so on. Almost every day, the ambassador receives personalities from the world of politics, economics, or culture for lunch or dinner. The cuisine prepared by the chef from Emilia Romagna is decidedly Italian, but he makes concessions to French taste in the shape, for example, of *foie gras* or a terrine. And surely there can be no better table in Paris for discovering the infinite variety of Italian wine. ❖

ABOVE LEFT *A dessert made by the residence's head cook.*
ABOVE RIGHT *A menu card emblazoned with the coat of arms of the Italian Republic.*
LEFT *On the ground floor, partial view of the Medardo Rosso Room that communicates through an arch to the main drawing room.*
FACING PAGE *On the first floor, the small dining room giving on the garden lends itself to less formal ambassadorial receptions.*
FOLLOWING PAGES *On the first floor to the court side. The Children's Games Room which owes its name to the various children's activities such as the swing, the seesaw, cup-and-ball, hot cockles, etc. that feature in the overdoors and which, together with the eighteenth-century gilded wood panels, are said to have come from the Château de Bercy (today Charenton-le-Pont). The room today serves as a venue for artistic events.*

ABOVE *Opening onto the garden, the Chinese Room was designed by decorator Adolfo Loewi from preexisting elements. On the ceiling, the coving is set off with arabesques with chinoiserie figures.*
FACING PAGE *A painted eighteenth-century* chinoiserie *panel showing a female figure retouched in the twentieth century by Venetian craftsmen and a French commode bearing the stamp of cabinetmaker BVRB, part of the eighteenth-century furniture that was brought to the residence during its refurbishment.*

FACING PAGE *The library seen from the garden. Through the eighteenth-century painted wooden archway one glimpses an Italian desk of the same period inlaid with architectural motifs in the 1930s. The fifteen landscapes ascribed to Vittorio Amedeo Cignaroli (1730–1800) were remounted by Adolfo Loewi into panels to form the dado.*

RIGHT *View through to the library from the Chinese room. Only the Louis XV fireplace and Versailles parquet flooring date from the time the residence was built.*

BELOW LEFT *The library: detail of one of the fifteen landscape paintings by Cignaroli comprising the dado.*

BELOW RIGHT *Detail of the library: a collection of books dating from the eighteenth century.*

FOLLOWING PAGES *The façade to the garden appears as it did originally: a sober eighteenth-century residence shorn of all "futility of ornament," as recommended by Jacques François Blondel (1705–1774), the great theoretician of classical French architecture.*

HÔTEL DE LA MARCK

·

RESIDENCE OF THE AMBASSADOR
OF THE KINGDOM OF BELGIUM

HÔTEL DE LA MARCK

RESIDENCE OF THE AMBASSADOR OF THE KINGDOM OF BELGIUM

Date of construction 1760

Architect Gilles Hiérosme Sandrié

SCARCELY TWO HUNDRED YARDS FROM THE ELYSÉE PALACE, IN THE UNPRETENTIOUS rue de Surène, stands a royal abode: the Hôtel de La Marck, the residence of the ambassador of Belgium, but also of the sovereign of the country whenever he (or she) comes on a private visit to France. Desirous of turning it into the country's embassy, Belgium acquired the building in 1935. By happy coincidence, it was built in about 1760 for Comte Louis Engelbert de La Marck, lieutenant-general in the king's army and governor of Cambrésis, who came from a great line of aristocrats with their main fief in the Hainaut. In 1951, the embassy and chancellery moved to rue de Tilsitt and the building became simply the residence of the ambassador.

Once through the double carriage-door, the building is preceded by a square court whose elegance and purity of line have been savored by two centuries of various owners and tenants. After the death of the Comte de La Marck, it was acquired by the Maréchal de Castries, Louis XVI's secretary of state to the navy, who rented it out to the Marquise de Chauvelin and then to the Duchesse de Deux-Ponts. The celebrated Marquis de La Fayette then became its owner, but he never really lived there either and so let it to François-Joseph de Choiseul-Meuse. Then, during the Second Empire, it belonged for fourteen years to the emperor's chamberlain, Comte de Mercy-Argenteau, a descendant of a great Belgian aristocratic family. At the beginning of the twentieth century, it became the property of the Comte de Pierre, a member of a noble and very ancient family originally from the Languedoc.

Today, the reception rooms offer visitors an impression of relative simplicity and majestic harmony. This feeling of ease derives not only from the tranquility and proportions of the halls, but also from calculated understatement: here, there are no stewards, even less a head of protocol. Once over the threshold, the guests, some of who will be requested to sign the visitors' book, are received in the great hall clad in white-and-gold wooden paneling of *rocaille* style. Another room is adorned with beautiful chinoiseries ascribed to the painter Jean-Baptiste Huet (1745–1811). Adjoining a small dining room for private meals—where one can see a splendid portrait signed by the Dutch painter Nicolas Maes (1632–1696)—one comes across the vast formal dining room that was created in the nineteenth century by opening several smaller rooms.

In this residence, a veneer of sobriety does not mean that strict rules of protocol are not observed. The ambassadress keeps to them, since she feels they facilitate the organization of the many receptions. Thus, for example, when the time comes to pass to table guests do not have to search around for their places but simply consult the seating plan. In a throwback to ancient tradition, the table is laid in the French style: the hosts are seated opposite one other at the center, the ambassador having the lady of the highest rank in terms of precedence to his right, while the ambassadress sits next to her male counterpart. To their left those of second rank take their place.

Once seated, guests can savor excellent French cuisine prepared by a chef from . . . Laos. The ambassadress has learned that it is best not serve warm entrées if a speech is planned for the beginning of the meal, nor a sorbet for dessert if one is expected at the conclusion of proceedings. Dinner is often a candlelit affair and guests are served on a Limoges porcelain service marked with the royal crown.

Official luncheons and dinners are held at irregular intervals. The calendar though features two important dates, when dozens, even hundreds of guests flock to a buffet: the national holiday, on July 21, to which a few hundred of the fifty thousand Belgians residing in France are invited; and November 15, King's Day, when the halls are crowded with celebrities of every nationality, friends from France, foreign diplomats, and Belgian officials. ❖

PRECEDING DOUBLE PAGE *View of the central staircase leading up to reception halls that present a subdued eighteenth-century decor.*
FACING PAGE *The main vestibule as seen by the ambassador's guests today was once a carriage entrance. The old carriage-door wall is hung with an eighteenth-century tapestry representing a scene of courtly love.*

ABOVE *To the garden side, a partial view of the large
salon whose rocaille eighteenth-century "white
and gold" wood trim proclaims its ceremonial
purpose. A seventeenth-century portrait of a lady
by the school of Van Dyck can also be seen.*
FACING PAGE *Garden side, a view of part of the small
dining room adorned with a portrait of a man
by the Dutch painter Nicolas Maes (1634–1693),
Rembrandt's most celebrated pupil. A rocaille
gilt-wood console table, from the eighteenth century,
here functions as a sideboard.*

FACING PAGE *The ambassador and his spouse like
to receive their guests in an anteroom that gives through
to the reception rooms that were altered in the nineteenth
century. Guests are requested to sign the visitor's book.
On either side of the door stand the 1843 portraits
of the Lieutenant-Generals Duvivier, by Van Ysendyck.*
ABOVE *Detail of a door to the main reception hall.*

LEFT *Detail of the Salon des Huet: one of four painted wooden panels.*
BELOW *The same Chinese-style room, with panels inserted in the gilded trim and original furniture upholstered in* petit point *tapestry depicting scenes from La Fontaine's Fables.*
FACING PAGE *Detail of the Chinese room: a tea scene. An example of the eighteenth-century taste for chinoiserie on one of the panels ascribed to Jean-Baptiste Huet (1745–1811).*

ABOVE *Detail in the small dining-room: tea is served.*
FACING PAGE *Garden side, the enfilade of reception rooms seen from the ceremonial dining room.*

ABOVE LEFT Glassware engraved with
the arms of the Kingdom of Belgium.
ABOVE RIGHT A guest napkin.
LEFT Fine porcelain employed
for receptions at the residence.
FACING PAGE The table is laid for an official
function in the ceremonial dining hall;
the room was ceated in the nineteenth century
from two smaller salons.

HÔTEL DE MONACO

·

RESIDENCE OF THE AMBASSADOR
OF THE REPUBLIC OF POLAND

HÔTEL
DE MONACO

RESIDENCE OF THE AMBASSADOR
OF THE REPUBLIC OF POLAND

Date of construction 1774–76
Architect Alexandre Théodore Brongniart

PAGE 156 *Constructed in the mid-nineteenth century, the ceremonial hall alone occupies the entire west wing of the residence.*
BELOW LEFT *Decoration in the original vestibule in the center of the main façade.*
BELOW RIGHT *Detail of the great hall in the west wing: a statue of Eve.*
FACING PAGE *A single-flight marble staircase built to the stipulations of the owner, the Dutch banker William Williams Hope. In 1841, the press was all abuzz with this "Croesus" moving into the "venerable" Faubourg Saint-Germain.*

"PERHAPS THE FINEST IN ALL THE FAUBOURG SAINT-GERMAIN," THE MARQUISE DE Breteuil said of the rooms in the Hôtel de Monaco. "The prettiest woman in France," proclaimed Horatio Walpole of the Princesse de Monaco, née Marie-Catherine de Brignole-Sale, for whom Alexander-Théodore Brongniart (1739–1813) built the residence. The heir to these two superlatives on rue Saint-Dominique is currently the residence of the ambassador of Poland. Its opulence would deserve many more accolades, just as its maintenance demands passion and immense care.

For the fabulously wealthy princess from Genoa, finally unshackled from her odious husband—Honoré III, sovereign-prince of Monaco—Brongniart decided to break with the customary neoclassic of Parisian residences and designed the vast house in the Italian style, complete with peristyle and nine windows to the front separated by Doric columns and extending into a terrace on the floor above.

Preceded by an avenue of plane trees and giving on to a delicious garden *à la française*, it nestles in greenery. Vestibule, great halls, dining room, library, the princess's private apartments—where her lover and neighbor the Prince de Condé would visit her every day—are all luxuriously appointed, but with the sobriety of the neo-Greek line, dispensing with the then fashionable *rocaille*. The couple, however, did not enjoy their commodious abode for long, being sent into exile in the early days of the Revolution.

Confiscated by the Republic, the Hôtel de Monaco was initially let out to the Ottoman ambassador, before falling into the hands of Abbé Sieyès, then member of the Directoire. In 1808, in the days of the Empire, it was sold to Maréchal Davout, who began to further embellish its decor, adding new furniture, pleated silk on the walls, and old master paintings. After his death, his widow rented it out to various States which one after the other employed it as their embassy.

The year 1826 witnessed the arrival of the Austrian ambassador, Count Anton Apponyi, the signal for a period of particular ostentation and social whirl. The count surprised and delighted all Paris by organizing singularly original balls: luncheon dances that kicked off at midday in the Viennese manner. A lover of literature and the arts, Apponyi frequently received writers such as Balzac and Musset, and liked to put on dazzling musical soirées. At one such, on December 30, 1832, after Kalkbrenner and Liszt had already caressed the ivories, a third man, young and unknown, strode to the piano. At last on the verge of worldwide fame, this pianist's name was Frederic Chopin.

In 1838, the Maréchale Davout sold the residence to the Dutchman William Williams Hope, heir to his father's colossal fortune, a banker whose name has gone down in the annals of history as the owner of a celebrated blue diamond. A significant art collector and confirmed bachelor with an eye for the ladies, Hope decided to transform the property completely: the main building was extended and then flanked by two large wings: one for outbuildings and service block, the other furnished with grandiose reception rooms.

Built by a pupil of Brongniart, Achilles-Jacques Fédel, this wing today remains one of the most dazzling interiors in Paris. The reception rooms are reached up a broad straight staircase in white marble worthy of a royal palace. The visit continues beneath a decor that is as opulent as it is eclectic, a mix of antiquity, Renaissance, and seventeenth century. The wonders scattered about the various rooms include ceiling paintings of Italian inspiration by Philippe Camairas (1803–1875), floral and still-life medallions decorating the ceiling in the banqueting hall, the fireplace in the ceremonial hall, and a piece by bronze-founder Pierre Maximilien Delafontaine (1774–1860) after drawings by Fédel.

The residence's luxury is so like Versailles that certain scenes from movies such as *The Supper* by Édouard Molinaro (1992) and Yves Simoneau's *Napoleon* (2002, with Christian Clavier) were filmed here.

Hope, a musician and music lover, did not forget to include a concert hall with excellent acoustics that is today often packed to the rafters. On Hope's death in 1855 the residence became the property of Baron Achille Seillière who bequeathed it to his daughter, Jeanne, wife of Talleyrand Périgord, Prince de Sagan. The princess, intelligent, elegant, and much-admired, turned it into a mecca for Parisian high society, throwing outlandish fancy-dress balls. Marcel Proust took her as a model for his Princesse de Parme. In 1909, the property was acquired by the art dealer Jacques Seligmann before, in 1935, being acquired by the Republic of Poland in exchange for the Hôtel du Cèdre at the foot of the Colline de Chaillot, where its legation was lodged but which the French government had allocated as the site for the Palais de Tokyo.

But what does this treasure trove of art history and Paris high-life represent for the Polish ambassadress of today? A responsibility whose burden can only be lightened by enthusiasm. She has to take care of the contents, as well as maintaining the building, preserving the works of art, and seeing to it that her guests enjoy their time here. Visitors can be counted in their thousands every year, often coming to one or other of the many concerts. The grand piano in the great hall will be played several dozen times during 2010, Chopin Year, before audiences of between a hundred and twenty and a hundred and forty, all also invited to a buffet.

Dinners given in the ground-floor dining room in the central building are more intimate. Up to twenty-two guests may assemble around a table laid beneath a splendidly decorated ceiling in coffered wood. The dishes, French or from the homeland according to circumstance, are prepared by the Polish chef and served on ivory-bordered, gold-edged white porcelain adorned with the Polish coat of arms. On other days, the ambassadress might prefer a Polish porcelain service with a Dutch-blue landscape motif. She designs her own menus and table decorations, and to ornament other rooms in the residence, she herself goes to the Rungis market outside of Paris to select her favorite blooms, peonies.

Not to show the glories of the Hôtel de Monaco to the largest possible audience would be unthinkable, so, on open days during the Journées du Patrimoine, as well as on Saturdays by request, the city hall of the seventh arrondissement organizes guided tours of the property. ❧

PRECEDING PAGES AND BELOW, TOP LEFT *The Blue Room: detail of the inlaid parquet floor. The Blue Room, a nineteenth-century creation inspired by the Versailles of Louis XIV, whose grandeur was in much vogue during Louis-Philippe's reign. Detail of the decoration on the ceiling.*

BELOW, TOP RIGHT *Detail of a door panel in the Blue Room. Sernik is a traditional cheesecake presented here with a summer topping.*

BOTTOM LEFT *Partial view through to the music room from the Blue room.*

BOTTOM RIGHT *The music room ceiling: detail of the baroque-style ornaments and of the medallions painted by Philippe Camairas (1803–1875), a pupil of Ingres.*

FACING PAGE *Leading through to the Blue Room, part of the music room where Franz Liszt would give piano recitals. It was here too that one evening in December 1832 Parisian society was to discover the genius of a young Frédéric Chopin. Today, the ambassador and his wife are pleased to allow Polish musicians to perform here, with an especial emphasis on Chopin in 2010, his bicentenary year.*

ABOVE LEFT *Detail of the dining room: the stand
of an nineteenth-century Polish silver centerpiece.*
ABOVE RIGHT *Detail of the table setting.*
LEFT *Porcelain made by the Slaska Manufactory
in Upper Silesia, produced as a tribute
to the Polish violinist and composer Henryk
Wieniawski (1835–1880).*
FACING PAGE *The table laid for an official function
in the ground-floor dining room that stands
on the former site of the formal apartments of
Marie-Catherine de Brignole-Sale—at the time
separated a mensa et thoro from the Prince
of Monaco—who, in the eighteenth century,
bought the land, building on it to be closer
to her lover, the Prince de Condé, who resided
in the Palais Bourbon, currently the French
National Assembly building.*

FACING PAGE *Detail of the garden: Rhythm, a work by Polish sculptor Henryk Kuna (1879–1945) that featured in the Polish Pavilion at the International Exhibition of Modern Decorative and Industrial Arts held in Paris in 1925.*
RIGHT *Perspective from the gate onto the main entrance with its antique peristyle.*
BELOW LEFT *View of the Eiffel Tower from the garden which, in the nineteenth century, stretched down to the esplanade at Les Invalides.*
BELOW RIGHT *Detail of the garden: a plant motif carved in stone.*

HÔTEL
DE PONTALBA

RESIDENCE OF THE AMBASSADOR OF
THE UNITED STATES OF AMERICA

HÔTEL DE PONTALBA

RESIDENCE OF THE AMBASSADOR OF THE UNITED STATES OF AMERICA

Dates of construction

1838–40
Baronne de Pontalba commissions from the architect Louis Visconti a private mansion on the site of a residence erected in the early eighteenth century.

1876–79
The Hôtel de Pontalba's new owner, Edmond de Rothschild, engages the architect Félix Langlais to overhaul the building, leaving intact just the gate to the street, the guardhouse, and the pediment with sculpture on the garden side.

PAGE 174 *The court front erected in 1878 by the architect appointed by the Rothschild family in accordance with the aesthetic canons of the first half of the eighteenth century.*

BELOW AND FACING PAGE *In the background, the entrance hall giving into the reception rooms opens onto the central courtyard. Hung above the main staircase, an equestrian portrait of George Washington. The main staircase, designed toward the end of the nineteenth century in a sober Louis XV style, leads to the Jefferson Library, the Lindbergh Room, and the bedroom of the President of the United States.*

THE HÔTEL DE PONTALBA SEEMS TO HAVE BEEN PREDESTINED TO BECOME THE residence of the United States ambassador to France. This elegant abode situated at 41, Faubourg Saint-Honoré was built at the end of the 1830s by an aristocrat of Spanish origin born in New Orleans where her father, a notary, had moved and made his fortune: Michaela Almonester y Roxas, Baronne de Pontalba.

Michaela's life was no dull affair. She had left her native Louisiana to settle in France with her husband, Baron Célestin Delfau de Pontalba, in the château possessed by the latter's father, Joseph, in the Oise. The couple's existence, punctuated by violent arguments, was not a happy one. In 1834, for some unknown reason, Baron Joseph Delfau de Pontalba fired a pistol at his daughter-in-law, wounding her rather seriously, before turning the weapon on himself. The event was soon regaling the Press.

The baroness was soon on the mend and started divorce proceedings, recovering both her independence and her fortune. As well as investing in real estate in New Orleans (where the Pontalba Apartments are now an historic building), by 1836 she had bought the house that a councilor to the court of the Parliament of Paris, Joseph-Antoine d'Aguesseau, had erected more than a century earlier at 41 rue du Faubourg Saint-Honoré. She decided to remodel it entirely, entrusting the task to a voguish architect of the day, Louis Visconti. Visconti, who created Napoleon's tomb at the Invalides during this same period, designed a residence of exemplary classicism, as shown today in the pediment on the garden side, the great entrance hall, and the gatehouse.

The baroness made a direct contribution to the works, reemploying several decorative elements to her taste saved from historic dwellings threatened by demolition, such as precious Chinese lacquer panels and wood decors from an aristocratic residence on rue de Lille then about to be razed. The whole residence was completed by the beginning of the 1840s, when the *baronne* started throwing sumptuous receptions for Paris high society.

Two years after her death, in 1874, the building was sold off by her heirs to the art lover and patron Edmond de Rothschild who called upon the services of another architect,

BELOW LEFT *Detail of the eighteenth-century Flemish tapestry illustrating a scene from the life of Moses, the Adoration of the Golden Calf, attributed to Gaspard van der Borght.*

BELOW RIGHT AND FACING PAGE *Opening on to the vestibule, the octagonal room was added at the demand of Baron Edmond de Rothschild (a perspicacious art collector) to house carved wainscoting with its magnificent rocaille ceiling ornaments, dating from the eighteenth century and originally from the Hôtel de Biron (today the Rodin Museum). Love, one of three paintings by William Bouguereau (1825–1905) a hugely popular painter during the Second Empire and the Third Republic, hangs in the vestibule.*

FOLLOWING PAGES *The Samuel Bernard Room, decorated (again on the initiative of Baron Edmond de Rothschild) with eighteenth-century wood panels from a private mansion in the Faubourg Saint-Germain-des-Prés. In 1740, this residence was the property of Jacques Samuel Bernard, finance minister to Louis XIV and Louis XV.*

Félix Langlais, to overhaul the building and add the two wings, the grand staircase, an octagonal *salon*, and several exquisite ensembles of old woodwork.

The decoration meanwhile was enriched by the baron's extraordinary collection of furniture and works of art, part of which he was to bequeath to various museums, including the Louvre. His son, Maurice, who inherited the residence shortly before the Second World War, managed to save some pieces before taking refuge in Switzerland. During the German Occupation, Herman Goering requisitioned the residence as an arm of the Nazis' Air Ministry. On the Liberation, Maurice de Rothschild recovered his property, as well as a proportion of the artworks looted by the Nazis but saved by the 7th Army of the United States. The Rothschilds then decided to rent Hôtel Pontalba to the British Royal Air Force Club, before selling it to the US Government in 1948.

The residence had over the years lost much of its luster and was shorn of the majority of old paneling and woodwork, the splendid ironwork on the staircase, and many other precious features, but it was deemed a suitable site for the embassy information unit and press office.

The situation appeared very different, however, when, in 1966, the US Government opted to turn it into a residence for its ambassador to France, and started a painstaking program of restoration, with, where necessary, the reuse of some of the original and long-vanished furnishings. The works began with the support of a group of American benefactors calling themselves the "Friends of 41," and was given new impetus beginning in 1972 under the tenure of Ambassador Arthur K. Watson. The Cultural Heritage Program continues to restore the house to its former magnificence.

The architects not only afforded it a new lease of life with these rejuvenated historic features, but also managed to incorporate many telling symbols of Franco-American friendship: a Jefferson Library and Franklin, La Fayette, and Lindbergh Rooms, all embellished with furniture, objects, and works evoking these great figures who had, in their different ways, strengthened links between the two nations.

Luckily enough, the Department of State, who had been very keen to replace the Chinese lacquer paneling the Baron of Pontalba had re-erected in her new home, later unearthed it, installing it in 2001 in the hall that today bears her name.

The site of the embassy of one of the world's most powerful nations has to cater for tens of thousands of people per year, a happy few being invited to dine in the great dining room with eighteenth-century wood paneling and hung with three vast Beauvais tapestries.

On fine days, American hospitality is plainly in evidence in the ample garden, particularly at the garden-party barbecue thrown on Independence Day, July 4. Specialties from many of the States of the Union are on hand, sometimes served *à la française* by the embassy's talented French *chef de cuisine*. A Gallic twist may even be given to such traditional Thanksgiving fare as pumpkin soup and apple pie. At the innumerable meals prepared throughout the year, he, however, also provides a panorama of French gastronomy, invariably preferring fresh, seasonal produce. ◈

FACING PAGE *The Louis XVI Room, lined with goldleaf skirting with so-called "Etruscan" motifs, testifies to the taste of elite society in the Baronne de Pontalba's time for Roman antiquity as reinterpreted by the ornemanistes of the eighteenth century. Of Parisian make, the gilt-bronze clock, with its case in the shape of a lyre, dates from the late eighteenth century.*

RIGHT *View of part of the Jefferson Library created in the 1970s in tribute to Thomas Jefferson, who, before becoming President, had served as the second American ambassador to France from 1785 to 1789. The armchair is the copy of a model drawn by Jefferson himself, while the collection of antiquarian books was assembled by William Short, Jefferson's personal secretary.*

BELOW LEFT *The Lindbergh Room boasts several souvenirs of the aviator who, on May 21, 1927, successfully flew non-stop across the North Atlantic aboard his Spirit of Saint Louis.*

BELOW RIGHT *Detail of the portrait of the Baroness Pontalba, c. 1840.*

FOLLOWING PAGES *The first-floor dining room decorated with Louis XV wainscoting is prepared for an official dinner. The mahogany table is ornamented with a set of silver figurines ordered in 1959 by President Eisenhower for a luncheon with General De Gaulle.*

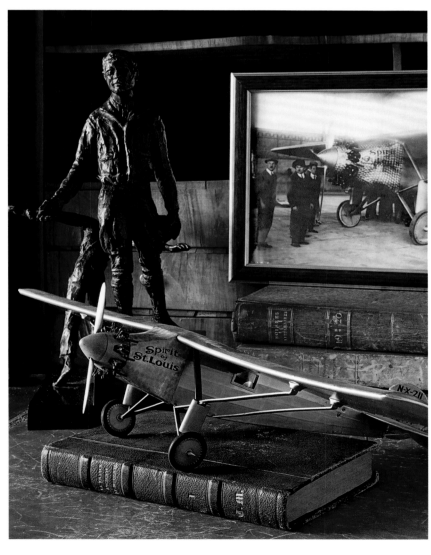

FACING PAGE AND ABOVE *The Pontalba Salon. The walls are decorated with precious Chinese lacquer panels from the eighteenth century that the Baroness Pontalba purchased from the home of the duchesse du Maine in Saint-Germain-des-Prés. The table is set for a small-scale official lunch celebrating Thanksgiving Day with Saint Louis crystal glass, Bernardaud porcelain from Limoges, Christofle silver, and Porthault table linens. The wine is by Opus One, a Bordeaux vintage grown in the Napa Valley. A perfect example of Franco-American cooperation.*

ABOVE LEFT, ABOVE RIGHT *Garden front. During celebrations for Independence Day on July 4, the Navy parades the Stars and Stripes. The façade is decked out in the American and French flags, recalling that France was the United States' very first ally.*
LEFT *The Fifes and Drums of Williamsburg, Virginia.*
FACING PAGE *On July 4, the American flags are deployed at the end of a side wing giving on to the garden.*
FOLLOWING PAGES *The garden front, graced by a pediment and by two wings, mirrors the court front built in the nineteenth century by Félix Langlais; only the carved pediment dates back to the eighteenth.*

HÔTEL DE BÉHAGUE

·

RESIDENCE OF THE AMBASSADOR
OF ROMANIA

HÔTEL
DE BÉHAGUE

RESIDENCE OF THE AMBASSADOR
OF ROMANIA

Dates of construction

1866–67

Initially, two mansions were edified:
one destined to Countess Amédée
de Béhague, and the other to her son Octave.

Architect Hippolyte Destailleur

1894–1905

These contructions were redesigned
and extended for Martine de Béhague.

Architect William Destailleur

THE HÔTEL DE BÉHAGUE ON RUE SAINT-DOMINIQUE, THE RESIDENCE OF THE
Romanian ambassador to France since 1939, is first and foremost an illustration of the
taste for beauty, of the culture and intelligence of the woman who commissioned its construction in 1893: Comtesse Martine de Béhague. An exceptional woman and immensely
wealthy, the countess cut a striking figure in Proust's Paris of the late nineteenth century,
and was friend to many of the literary luminaries of the age.

Martine de Béhague had inherited the site from her grandmother Amédée who had
erected it in 1866. The old countess, unique heiress to a stockbroker and peer of France,
had acquired the land and ordered the then famous architect, Hippolyte Destailleur, to
build a vast mansion for herself, and another, smaller one, for her son Octave, the whole
in the Louis XV style of which she was especially fond.

These constructions, however, did not greatly please the flamboyant Martine, who
decided to build a new, still more majestic residence more to her taste on the very spot
where the previous ones had stood. On their demolition, she called upon Destailleur's
son, William, to realize her own project, no less inspired by the eighteenth century. The
acquisition of the intervening plot made room for the most impressive component of the
residence: a concert hall, built by Gustave-Adolphe Gerhardt, that remains to this day
the largest private theater of its kind in Paris.

Of Byzantine inspiration, resembling a church illumined by the daylight that floods
in through the sliding roof, and complete with an orchestra pit and the largest organ
case in private hands in Paris, this room, which is tabled for restoration soon, is simply
astonishing. A serpentine staircase makes it possible to reach it from the entrance, while
from her box Martine de Béhague could descend directly to the foyer where she would
meet up with friends during the interval.

The other highlight in this exceptional building is the oval-shaped, all-wood library,
fitted with library stairs on casters that slide along a handrail, trompe l'oeil-painted
iron shades to protect the books from sunlight, and an impressive collection of valuable
tomes assembled by the countess's private librarian and friend, the poet Paul Valéry.

The splendor and originality of some of the other architectural and decorative elements are breathtaking: one opulently carved wooden staircase led to the countess's
private apartments, today the ambassador's office; the grand Versailles-inspired staircase in polychrome marble; a large bas-relief decorating the marble-clad hall showing
Time Abducting Love and signed by the sculptor Jean Dampt; the huge dining room also
clad in marble and adorned by a monumental canvas by François Boucher, *The Birth of
Venus*; the great *salon*, all blue and gold, embellished with some extraordinary Louis XV
wood paneling; and not forgetting the elegant frontages of a preeminently pure French
classicism that can be seen from the court and garden.

PAGE 192 *Opening onto the main courtyard, the
vestibule—with its vaulted arches and red-and-
white marble paving—was furbished at the end
of the nineteenth century by the architect
William Destailleur, commissioned by the owner
Martine de Béhague. On one side, the hall leads
to the great gallery that opens onto the garden
and on the other to the private concert hall
that gives on to rue Saint-Dominique.*
RIGHT *The great gallery—in white stone, fronting
the garden—leads to a large marble-lined
staircase. Today, the gallery is the habitual
venue for cultural events organized jointly by the
ambassador and the Romanian Cultural Institute.*
FACING PAGE *In a great court, oval in shape,
the broad stone portico in front of the entrance
hall sheltered the countess's guests as they
stepped out of their vehicles.*

Romania, historically, culturally, and emotionally so close to France, is a worthy custodian of this jewel. For twenty years, ambassadors have striven to forget the long years considered so dark both by their French friends and by those of the sizable Romanian community residing in France, composed mainly of people exiled during the dictatorship.

Throughout the year, various events are organized that make a building long closed to the outside world throb with life. The auditorium is once again open for concerts, films, and frequent stage performances: musicians, composers, directors, and authors from the homeland are frequently invited to appear before French and Romanian guests alike. The great hall, which can seat as many as a hundred, is another venue for many activities, sometimes organized in collaboration with the Romanian Cultural Institute: from fashion shows to symposia, from concerts to seminars, and exhibitions. It is here, for example, that in 2008 took place the official launch of the ELI (Extreme Light Infrastructure) project financed by the European Commission that envisages the construction by 2013–15 of a powerful ultra laser that should pave the way for an entirely novel physics. In a completely different domain, 2009 saw the launch of a major biography of playwright Eugène Ionesco by André Gall, published by Flammarion. Other events provide opportunities for genial get-togethers, such as the Romanian national festival on December 1, to which more than two thousand people may be invited, or the yearly gathering of the more than six hundred Romanian students and researchers residing in France.

Affording a backdrop of great beauty, parts of the residence are sometimes hired out for movie shoots (certain scenes of *La Vie en Rose* [*La Môme*] by Olivier Dahan were filmed here, as well as Proust's *À la Recherche du Temps Perdu*, directed by Nina Companeez) or by organizations desirous of holding some truly memorable event. ❖

FACING PAGE AND ABOVE *View of part of the dining room,*
also clad in colored marble, inspired by the Grand Siècle
style created by Charles Le Brun for The Sun King.
To the left, a green jasper niche containing a baroque-style
fountain decorated with a grotesque mask and a conch
can be seen. Nowadays, the room is dedicated to official
functions as well as to diplomatic meetings.

PRECEDING PAGES *Detail of the dining room clad with marble and stone. Directly opposite the baroque fountain, The Birth of Venus, dated 1731, one of the earliest forays of François Boucher (1703–1770), demonstrates the quality of the collection assembled by the Comtesse de Béhague for the building. As Gabriele D'Annunzio once wrote to her: "Tomorrow, Monday, I will come to lunch in Fragonard's park."*

FACING PAGE *The library, of oval form, paneled entirely in the eighteenth century and with a ceiling painted with an allegory, Dawn Chasing away the Darkness, gives onto the garden. A ladder on casters running along a rail made it easier for poet Paul Valéry to consult its precious holdings when he worked as Martine de Béhague's librarian.*

RIGHT *Detail of some eighteenth-century direct carving on a wooden door panel on the first storey.*

BELOW LEFT *Detail of the library: this delicately carved door communicates with the hall to the private apartments.*

BELOW RIGHT *Detail of the library: just a few of the rare editions of the nineteenth and twentieth centuries collected by Martine de Béhague with assistance from her librarian, Paul Valéry.*

PAGE 204 *The wooden stairwell, surmounted by a glass canopy, is lined entirely in eighteenth-century waxed oak paneling. The banister is composed of various eighteenth-century Flemish and French carved balusters. The whole ensemble was the brainchild of the architect William Destailleur.*

PAGE 205 *View of the vestibule and the wooden staircase that leads up to the countess's private apartments that serve today as offices for the ambassador. Beneath the stairs can just be seen a door in carved wood concealing Martine de Béhague's still-operational personal elevator.*

LEFT, BELOW LEFT, AND BELOW RIGHT *The Gold Room, detail of the elaborate paneling and false mirror-glass doors. The Gold Room, view to the garden side. This salon now hosts piano recitals. In the same salon, a detail of rocaille-style wood on the walls.*

FACING PAGE *Dominating the garden, the Salon Doré is a reconstitution in pure rocaille style of fragments taken from historic residences demolished during Baron Haussmann's development work in Paris. This room reflects Martine de Béhague's interest in eighteenth-century decorative art. Today it is a venue for conferences and cultural events.*

BELOW *Detail of the small octagonal room: L'Hallali, one of the four eighteenth-century hunting scenes on canvas.*
FACING PAGE *The small octagonal salon with beeswaxed wood and mirror-glass doors sits between the dining room and the Gold Room.*

PAGE 210 *TOP, LEFT AND RIGHT* Detail of the concert hall: wrought-iron door panel giving through to the wings and gold-backed mosaic. *BOTTOM* The largest private concert hall in Paris commissioned by Martine de Béhague from Gustave-Alolphe Gerhardt in a style inspired by Byzantine decoration. The decoration of the columnade is inspired by Oriental churches. The porphyry columns alternate with plaques framed in gold-ground mosaic. In what was an innovation for the time, the space is lit by an open dome. Gabriel Fauré directed his Requiem here, Camille Saint-Saens and Charles-Marie Widor also performed here. In 1909, the dancer Isadora Duncan performed here; sculptor Auguste Rodin was in the audience. *PAGE 211* View of the concert hall from the portico perpendicular to the stage whose columns and capitals are inspired by Byzantine models. *LEFT* An antique-style pediment marks the end of the garden, planted in the French style, which extends from rue Saint-Dominique to rue de Grenelle. Before the development of the new Paris during the Second Empire, this historic district, known as "Gros-Caillou," was occupied by craftsmen and market gardeners. *BELOW* The garden front was erected in 1902 in the purest seventeenth- and eighteenth-century French architectural tradition, following the manner of the paired Palais Gabriel on the Place de la Concorde. *FACING PAGE* On the first floor the reception rooms open through to an exterior gallery supported by a portico over eight ionic columns giving onto the garden.

HÔTEL
LANDOLFO-
CARCANO

—————— • ——————

RESIDENCE OF THE AMBASSADOR
OF THE STATE OF QATAR

HÔTEL LANDOLFO-CARCANO

RESIDENCE OF THE AMBASSADOR OF THE STATE OF QATAR

Date of construction 1868
Architect Charles Rohault de Fleury

QATAR HOSPITALITY OBEYS RULES THAT ARE AS INTANGIBLE AS THEY ARE EXQUISITE: on one's arrival, the guest is engulfed in a cloud of sweet-smelling incense rising from a traditional *oud*—a stick of scented wood smoldering away in a brazier—and then, once seated comfortably in the drawing room, he is invited to take coffee. This is the manner in which the ambassador of the State of Qatar and his wife like to receive guests, not only in their private residence in the sixteenth arrondissement but also in the Hôtel Landolfo-Carcano, a building between the rue de Tilsitt and the place de l'Étoile which has been the seat of the embassy since 2007. The ambassadors of Qatar have occupied this undemonstrative mansion near the Porte Dauphine quarter since 2003, the year that saw the building refitted and redecorated in the spirit of the homeland—that is, with unabashed modernity blended with discreet but far from token nods to a long heritage.

Thus, at the entrance on the ground floor, the scented visitor discovers at once preeminently modern abstract collages by Qatari artist Yusef Ahmed and, at the foot of the staircase, a neat, typically Bedouin room with low seats adorned in colorful geometrical motifs and storage trunks. At one time imported from the Indies or from Zanzibar, these more or less lavishly decorated teakwood coffers were used as "safes" for the family's most valuable property. Today they make charming decorative features.

An elevator conducts the visitor directly to the second floor (the first is strictly private), containing the great hall and the dining room. The perfume of incense continues to accompany his visit in the salon as he takes his place on one of the nine couches covered in golden canvas. No more than a score of guests are received here, larger receptions being held at the embassy. The golden yellow walls are hung with canvases one might term "Orientalist" were they not the work of a Qatari artist: pearl-fishing boats, cavalcades, and camels in the desert reinforce the exotic ambience.

As soon as he sits down, the visitor is again offered the inevitable cup of coffee, a firm fixture in Qatari hospitality, and in the Arab world generally. The manner in which the coffee pot is poured and the cups are held, how the beverage is drunk and the cup shaken (or not) once drained . . . everything is carefully codified, everything possesses a precise meaning with nothing left to chance. Only mildly roasted, the coffee is flavored with cardamom and saffron. No sugar is taken, but the brew is accompanied by dates.

PAGE 214 *The main front of the Hôtel Landolfo-Carcano looking over to the Arc de Triomphe. It is one of twelve Second Empire "Hôtels des Maréchaux" erected from 1860 to 1868. Promoted by Napoleon III, who desired that its new layout pay homage to Emperor Napoleon I.*
PRECEDING DOUBLE PAGES *The hall of honor giving on the rue de Tilsit still displays its Napoleon III-style architectural decor created in 1868. The monograms of Marquis Landolfo-Carcano and his wife Anne-Marie Caussin—the residence's first owner—appear on the columns and antique pilasters that punctuated the marble-encrusted vestibule.*
RIGHT *A detail of the ceiling fresco in the grand salon,* the Triumph of Juno.
FACING PAGE *On the first floor. Contiguous to the ambassador's private office, the great room opening on the Arc de Triomphe, which conserves its original decoration and furniture, has benefited from a lengthy restoration program from 2005 to 2007. The center of the ceiling is embellished with an oval fresco on the mythological theme of the* Triumph of Juno *signed by the decorative painter Alexis-Joseph Mazerolle.*
FOLLOWING DOUBLE PAGES *On the first floor. In the southwest wing addressing the avenue des Champs-Élysées, the great dining room—with its coffered ceiling painted with arabesques, overmantle flanked by carved wood caryatids, and two Italian-style curio cabinets—presents a neo-Renaissance decor rehabilitated in the course of the Second Empire. In the present day, the reception room acts as a backdrop for signings of bilateral agreements, official functions, and seminars.*

Once this ritual is completed, guests are invited to pass to table. The dining room contains four small tables of six covers. Here too the traditions—culinary this time—are respected: just as in Doha, roast lamb (instead of mutton), fish, and shrimps, accompanied by spiced rice, are the dishes most usually served. In what is a necessary concession to Western lifestyles, food is served *à la française,* though the tablecloths and napkins are embroidered with *sadu* motifs, a traditional yet living art among the Bedouin of the Arabian Peninsula.

Lastly, after one further coffee and before saying farewell to their hosts and leaving the residence, in a Qatari custom faithfully observed in the heart of Paris, guests are invited to choose one of the fragrances on a tray and perfume themselves.

This is how diplomats from all nations, delegations from the State, or French friends of Qatar (a numerous body as the significant French presence in the country testifies) are received at the residence of the ambassador of Qatar for lunch or dinner, at a rate of several times a week.

Multinational companies rub shoulders with subsidiaries of the Institut Pasteur, and graduates of the Saint-Cyr military school with MBAs from the H.E.C. international business school. Two French high schools, the Lycée Bonaparte and the Lycée Voltaire, cater for the residents' children. And all enjoy the Qatar spirit of tolerance, liberality, and Francophilia. Language courses at the French Cultural Center in Doha are full to bursting. But it is not only eminent figures who are received, it is one of the few diplomatic residences that organizes every year on the 14th of the month of Ramadan a party for children. It takes place after the *iftar,* the hour when the fast can be broken at sunset, and honors the Qatari custom of *garangao,* when, in former times, children dressed in traditional costume would gather in small groups and visit houses in their neighborhood to ask for treats.

This children's festival today tends to be celebrated in the family, with close relations or friends. On the evening in question, the ambassadress thus welcomes the great family of the Qatari children in France, accompanied by their many friends, for what is invariably the most joyous reception of the year. ❖

FACING PAGE *Detail of the Hall of Honor: the Bedouin-style corner—boasting wool items woven with characteristic colors and geometrical patterns—was arranged by the ambassador's wife. At one time, each Qatari family would have possessed one or more teak-wood trunks with copper fittings, used to store important documents, jewelry, and special garments. An oud, a sweet-smelling stick of sandalwood, burns away on a small portable brazier next to flasks for Oriental perfumes of sandalwood, myrrh, amber, and jasmine.*

ABOVE LEFT AND RIGHT *The first rule of hospitality in a Qatari household is to offer a date and a cardamom-spiced coffee to guests who enter the door.*

HÔTEL BERTHIER DE WAGRAM

RESIDENCE OF THE AMBASSADOR
OF THE KINGDOM OF SPAIN

HÔTEL BERTHIER DE WAGRAM

RESIDENCE OF THE AMBASSADOR OF THE KINGDOM OF SPAIN

Dates of construction

1869
A neoclassic building was edified for a wine merchant from Bordeaux, Nathaniel Johnston.

1894
Berthe Claire de Rothschild, Princesse de Wagram, bought a parcel of land so as to extend and embellish the existing house (a garden was created and a ballroom was added).
Architect Stéphane Le Bègue

IN PARIS, AT THE END OF THE NINETEENTH CENTURY, THE BALLS GIVEN BY THE Princesse de Wagram in her private mansion on avenue d'Alma (today, avenue George V) were among the most lavish of all. At the same time, near the place de Étoile, there was also held what was called the "bal Wagram," a very different affair to which servants and waiters would flock on their nights out. Marcel Proust, in a foreword to a book written late in life by the painter Jacques-Émile Blanche, tells an amusing anecdote from his youth. Still very timid, he used to conceal the fact that he ventured into the world of high society from his schoolfellows. One day when he was in the bus on his way to a ball thrown by the Princesse de Wagram (his father didn't like to pay his hackney carriage fare), he met a friend who noticed he was wearing formal dress under his overcoat and asked him where he might be going in such a get-up. Afraid to say he was off to a ball given by a princess, but not wanting to materially lie either, Proust replied that he was going to the "bal Wagram," without knowing what it was nor what kind of people went there, resulting in much hilarity on the part of his young friend. It was perhaps that very same evening—since it was at a ball given by the princess on July 1, 1893—that Proust saw for the first time a woman who was to leave an enduring mark on his life and work, the sublime Comtesse Greffulhe—the principal model for the fictional Duchesse de Guermantes.

The Princesse de Wagram's ballroom still exists and on occasion elegant receptions are given there, though the building long ago changed owners: on November 6, 1920, the Spanish State acquired it from the princess's children and grandchildren to convert into the nation's embassy to France.

The building had been erected in 1869 for Nathaniel Johnston, a wealthy Bordeaux wine merchant. The site of the property extended from the avenue d'Alma to avenue Joséphine (now avenue Marceau), thoroughfares that had been opened up only a decade previously. The architect respected the precepts of Haussmann, erecting a French Classical-style building over two floors surmounted by a mansard roof and appointed with a vast and splendid garden.

The Johnston family sold it in 1891 to Berthe Claire de Rothschild, wife of the third Prince de Wagram, a descendant of Berthier, marshal during the Empire. A year after acquiring it, the Spanish State embarked on important modernization and restoration works. By June 22, 1923, the Embassy could be installed in its new premises. One of the most richly decorated residences in all Paris, its upper floors were reserved for administrative and political bureaus, while the lower floors served as the scene for the more ceremonial activities.

Since all the administrative services and the chancellery were transferred to modern buildings constructed to the avenue Marceau side in 1992, what visitors discover today is practically a museum piece. Since 1923, the larger ballroom, occupying the whole width of the residence between the avenue George V and the garden, has been decorated entirely in splendid tapestries woven by the Royal Manufacture of Santa Barbara in 1794 from cartoons of Goya showing typical scenes of Madrid life such as a fair, market, and games. The immense carpet, with its motifs inspired by the decorative *boiseries* on the walls, was made to measure, as is the case in all other rooms in the building. As evening falls, the shutters are closed to reveal a revetment of mirrors.

PAGE 226 *View of the stateroom from the vestibule. Portrait of King Alfonso XIII by José Llaneces (1863–1919), the sovereign who in 1920 gave permission to acquire the building as the country's embassy.*
FACING PAGE *Detail of the anteroom: eighteenth-century chest of drawers with the marks of Pierre II Migeon (c. 1637–1677).*

As for the interior of the ceremonial dining room, it is entirely by the hand of José Maria Sert, the renowned Catalan painter and decorator, an eminent member of the interwar artistic and cultural life in Paris, one of whose muses was his first wife, the socialite Misia Sert. He filled the sumptuous dining-hall with spectacular black marble and an important collection of eighteenth-century tapestries on the theme of Don Quixote from the Royal Manufacture in Madrid, after cartoons by Andrea Procaccini.

The table can be extended to seat as many as thirty-eight diners. The service is of Bidassoa porcelain and is laid on silver platters. The glassware is Baccarat crystal. Pedro, majordomo here for a quarter of a century, keeps a watchful eye over the seating arrangements, while the two chefs—one Italian and the other Spanish—man the kitchens which still display many of their original nineteenth-century fittings.

The various rooms play host to frequent functions. Important events take place on the king's feast day, June 24, when five hundred Spanish personalities are invited, as well as on the national holiday, October 12, when the ambassador receives more than eight hundred French guests. But the residence is used even more frequently for informal meetings, working lunches, for example, around a table set in the smoking room.

Visitors may then take the opportunity of walking round the various salons looking at their thousand and one treasures including old masters on loan from the Prado. There is a significant collection of royal portraits from the sixteenth to the twentieth century, together with various works by painters of the caliber of Pantoja de la Cruz, Sofonisba Anguisciola, and Bassano; valuable furniture including a Louis XIV gaming table in the Throne Room, two Louis XV commodes in an anteroom, and two seventeenth-century Spanish traveling chests. The visitor might miss, perhaps, the interior of an intimate chapel, ensconced down a staircase, dedicated to the Virgin of Covadonga and decorated with a striking triptych of the *Deposition* by José Maria Sert. ❖

ABOVE LEFT *The ceremonial dining room:
detail of the eighteenth-century Don Quixote tapestry.*
ABOVE RIGHT *Detail of one of the tapestries illustrating
the further adventures of Don Quixote de la Mancha
from the book by Miguel de Cervantes (1547–1616),
woven in 1744 by the Royal Manufacture of Madrid
to an order from King Philip V.*
LEFT *Detail of a table setting for an official meal.*
FACING PAGE *The ceremonial dining room looking on the
garden. The current interior was designed in the 1920s
by the Catalan painter José Maria Sert (1874–1945):
the black marble wall revetment and the pink marble
consoles form a backdrop to six wall-hangings
illustrating the story of Don Quixote. The carpet was
commissioned from the Royal Manufacture at Madrid.*

FACING PAGE *Enfilade of reception rooms seen from the ceremonial dining room.*
RIGHT *A traditional dish as served at the residence: paella marinera, with Galician shellfish.*
BELOW LEFT *Manufactured in Bidassoa, the residence's porcelain service is stamped with the arms of Charles III of Spain.*
BELOW RIGHT *Menu card on a table laid for an official meal.*

Dîner du 23 juillet

Piquillos farcis aux fruits de mer

Perdrix à l'étouffé

« Tocino de Cielo »

Albariño Martín Codax
Marqués de Riscal Gran Reserva 1994
Cava Codorníu Raventós

BELOW *The corridor giving through to the main rooms leads to the ballroom. To the rear, a bust of 1924 of King Alfonso XIII by the sculptor Mariano Benlliure (1862–1947).*
FACING PAGE *Partial view of the ballroom that contains four eighteenth-century hangings woven by the Royal Manufacture of Santa Barbara, after cartoons by Goya and presented to the residence by King Alfonso XIII. Marcel Proust (1871–1922) often came to balls given by the Princesse de Wagram in this turn-of-the-century decor.*

ABOVE *Detail of the ballroom with* The Fair at Madrid, *one of four tapestries executed after cartoons by Goya illustrating scenes of daily life in Madrid.*

FACING PAGE *Detail of the ballroom with* The Dance, *showing another of Goya's favorite themes of popular life in late eighteenth-century Madrid.*

PAGE 242 *Detail of the oratory: a replica of the Virgin of Covadonga, originally from a monastery in the Asturias.*

PAGE 243

TOP LEFT *Detail of the embroidered velvet over the altar of the Virgin of Covadonga from northern Spain.*

TOP RIGHT *Detail of the triptych* The Deposition *by the painter José Maria Sert (1874–1945) hanging on one of the oratory walls.*

BOTTOM *View of the oratory at the heart of the residence, an original work by José Maria Sert from the 1920s.*

HÔTEL LAFONT DE LA VERNÈDE

RESIDENCE OF THE AMBASSADOR
OF THE REPUBLIC OF PERU

HÔTEL LAFONT DE LA VERNÈDE

RESIDENCE OF THE AMBASSADOR OF THE REPUBLIC OF PERU

Date of construction 1880

Architect Julien Bayard

Beautiful examples of architecture, the *hôtels particuliers* of Paris that have remained embalmed in their original decor and thus invite one on a journey through time, can also offer a moving spectacle. This is the case with the residence located on avenue Kléber at the corner with rue Paul Valéry that is today the seat of the Peruvian embassy in France and the abode of the country's ambassador.

Erected in 1880 by the architect Julien Bayard for the Lafont family of Vernède, it was sold in 1912 to a M. de Miero, the ambassador of Uruguay, who had the building refitted. Three years later, it was ceded to M. Mimbela, the ambassador of Peru. The Peruvian State finally acquired the premises together with its furniture from his daughter-in-law in 1957 and it was listed as an historical building in 2004.

From the high windows of a small hall furnished with fine copies in Louis XV and Louis XVI style, in line with rue Hamelin where Marcel Proust lived and died, one can see the Eiffel Tower almost in its entirety. To another side, the same salon gives on rue Paul Valéry, where this other great writer also worked and died. In this unaltered decor, the ghosts of these writers evoke a Paris long lost. Visitors would be excused for indulging in nostalgic reverie, were it not that the embassy is a bustling, forward-looking place, full of life.

One little-known fact can help one understand why the embassy is such a hive of activity: in terms of student numbers the Alliance Française in Lima is the largest in the world. For young Peruvians show a keen interest in French language and culture, and the Paris embassy is their crucible. Just recently it played host to no fewer than twenty-one university vice-chancellors in an effort to boost the numbers of students from Peru coming to France.

The embassy also tries to offer the French a better knowledge of the homeland. More than once a month are organized what are dubbed "Peruvian conversations," when a hundred chairs are laid out in the gallery and two or three figures (it was recently the turn of the great Peruvian writer Mario Vargas Llosa) are invited to an open discussion on a vast range of subjects—history, economics, politics, or art.

On a regular basis, the ambassador and his wife organize breakfast meetings, lunches, and dinners for special guests from France and Peru alike: businessmen are briefed before visiting Peru; artists come to Paris for the annual festival of Peruvian cinema; and, naturally, Peruvian ministers and MPs on a visit to France are catered for as well. The Head of State and the head of the government each dispose of their own apartment on site.

PAGE 244 *Detail of the main vestibule: the staircase (a national heritage monument) rises to a great gallery on the first floor leading to the reception rooms that give on the avenue Kléber.*
RIGHT *Detail of a scroll in the main staircase.*
FACING PAGE *Detail of one end of the great gallery: the loggia, decorated in the late nineteenth century, is still used by musicians. Today, the great gallery serves as a venue for conferences, debates, and "Peruvian conversations" centered on notable intellectual figures.*

On the ground floor, a small atrium of stucco and russet marble preludes some fine *fin de siècle* interiors, underlined by a sky motif above by Horace de Callias (1847–1921), who painted most of the ceilings in the building.

Designated as an historic monument by the City of Paris due to its elegance and the beauty of its ironwork, the staircase leads to the gallery, where, as well as columns in stucco and gold-leaf gilded paneling, one can admire large Sèvres vases and some impressive floral-patterned stained glass dating to 1926, by the master glassmaker, Charles Champigneulle.

On a Louis XVI table, the ambassador and his wife have chosen to place some lavish, distinctively Peruvian repoussée-decorated baroque silverware (Peru is the greatest silver producer in the world), including baptismal basins in the shape of a shell, a traveling trunk called a *bargueño*, and another, smaller shell for visiting cards. Solid silver objects in the same style can be found in the great *salon* and the dining room. The gallery is equipped with a loggia, often filled at the time of major receptions with musicians.

With its black marble columns and outsized gilded chandelier, the dining-room decor is most impressive. Around a table with flowers arranged by the ambassadress herself, between solid silver candlesticks and centerpieces in the shape of angels, guests can savor choice dishes of Peruvian cuisine, one of the most sophisticated on the planet. Woefully neglected, it has recently begun to find favor all over the world. The Peruvian chef delights diners with the great specialties of his country, among which *cebiche*, one of many recipes of raw fish marinated in lemon juice and other ingredients; *aji de gallina*, a creamy preparation of chicken and pepper; or else *chupe de camaroñes*—a thick soup with gambas or crayfish.

Served at every cocktail party thrown at the embassy, the famous and eminently tasty drink called *pisco sour*—a grape-based aquavit, mixed in a shaker with lemon, egg white, sugar syrup, and ice—equally appreciated as an aperitif, celebrates the friendship between host nation and homeland. ❖

FACING PAGE *View of part of the great hall
that opens into the dining room.*
BELOW *View of the dining room from the great gallery.
The table is set for an official dinner beneath
a sky-painting by Horace de Caillas (1847–1921).*
FOLLOWING PAGES *The dining room. The table is set
for an official function.*

جمهورية مصر العربية

HÔTEL
EPHRUSSI

———— • ————

**RESIDENCE OF THE AMBASSADOR
OF THE ARAB REPUBLIC OF EGYPT**

HÔTEL
EPHRUSSI

RESIDENCE OF THE AMBASSADOR
OF THE ARAB REPUBLIC OF EGYPT

Date of construction date 1886–87

Architect Ernest Sanson

ANYONE WHO HAS SAVORED EGYPTIAN HOSPITALITY ON THE BANKS OF THE NILE will be agreeably unsurprised by the generosity and delicacy with which one is received in Paris at the residence of the Egyptian ambassador to France.

Located on the place des Etats-Unis—one of the finest squares in all Paris, ringed by splendid mansions—this was once the private abode of Jules Ephrussi. A banker, aesthete, and collector originally from Odessa, Ephrussi had called upon the talents of one of the most feted architects of the time: Ernest Sanson. His taste for traditional elegance and a concern to provide his customers with the modern comforts made his one of the favorite practices of the aristocracy and wealthier haute bourgeoisie.

As such he was responsible for many extensions and restorations of châteaus and also for dozens of splendid private dwellings in Paris. Among them was the famous Palais Rose for Boni de Castellane on avenue Foch (tragically demolished at the end of the 1960s), the Hôtel de Noailles again on the place des États-Unis, and the Broglie residence, rue de la Bienfaisance.

In spring 1886, work started on a site measuring 931m² that Ephrussi had acquired at the corner of the square—recently created after the Passy reservoirs were demolished— and avenue d'Iéna. In keeping with his penchant for the classical, Sanson designed the residence in the Louis XVI style. Behind an imposing carriage door of elegant concave form, the double-pile residence is arranged around a beautiful grand courtyard. The façade is fronted with Ionic pilasters.

Jules Ephrussi and his Austrian wife, née Fanny von Pfeiffer, died childless within a few months of each another in 1915. Thirteen years later, on an official visit to France, King Fuad I of Egypt bought the mansion as a residence for the very first Egyptian ambassador to Paris. At the time of his stay, the king also purchased the embassy building, on 56 avenue d'Iéna. Great Britain had granted the independence of its Nile protectorate relatively recently in 1922. The first ambassador in Paris, who arrived in 1924, was one of the king's sons-in-law, Mahmoud Fakhry Pacha, husband of Princess Fawkia. After leaving the suite they had occupied for a few years at the Hotel Majestic on rue Perugia, the couple settled in the superb mansion, occupying it for more than twenty years: Mahmoud Pasha Fakhry only left his posting in 1948.

PAGE 256 *The courtyard front of the Hôtel Ephrussi erected in 1886 in a new district near the Arc de Triomphe.*
RIGHT *The spiral staircase serves the rooms reserved for official guests, together with the library of King Farouk.*
FACING PAGE *Partial view of the hall of honor with a loggia designed by Paul Ernest Sanson, an architect much in vogue in the Belle Époque whose art is impregnated with eighteenth-century classicism and who was also responsible for Boni de Castellane's famous Palais Rose.*
FOLLOWING PAGES *The ground-floor dining room is decorated with friezes and painted arabesques adorned with flowers and enlivened with imaginary birds. The table is set in the French style around an evocative centerpiece: an oasis scene composed by the ambassador's wife.*

The building remained in the hands of the Egyptian State after the revolution of 1952, preserving its function as an ambassadorial residence. In 1996 and 1997, it was overhauled and its architectural splendors given a fresh lick of paint. At the turn of the century, the ambassadress planned to restore much of the furniture. Inside, its regal splendors seem to have survived intact: the apartment of King Farouk, for example, including chamber, bathroom, and drawing-room-library, has survived the half-century of the Republic quite unscathed. In the salons, pictures by Egyptian artists and "Egyptomaniac" works of art—such as the two Egyptian women among a collection of biscuit china in a showcase—discreetly evoke the banks of the Nile against what is an essentially eighteenth-century backdrop.

Numerous functions are held here, particularly since the foundation in 2008 of the Union for the Mediterranean, co-chaired by President Hosni Mubarak: Egyptian ministers, parliamentary delegations, diplomats, and businessmen passing through Paris for work meetings or to sign agreements frequently cross these hallowed portals. Forty guests can be served together at four tables erected in the dining room. The dishes prepared by the Egyptian chef, who has trained in various cuisines including French, are served on a service emblazoned with the eagle, symbol of the Arab Republic of Egypt.

The ambassador and his wife like to receive "as at home," and hold informal get-togethers between people from very different walks of life: artists, diplomats, and businessmen all rub shoulders in a cordial environment presided over by the great Egyptian qualities of warmth and humor. These characteristics come to the fore at the sumptuous *iftar*—the meal that signals the end of the fast of Ramadan—held at the residence every year. ❖

Voyage Gustatif en Egypte

*Assiette orientale composée :
feuilles de vignes farcies, «bessara» et «tamia»*
***
*« Fattet Magdous »
Assiette orientale aux aubergines, pignons et
viande hachée avec sa sauce au yaourt épicé*
***
*Assiette de grillades orientales marinées :
brochettes de «kofta», côtelettes d'agneau
riz à l'orientale aux amandes et raisins secs*
***
Dessert oriental « Om Ali aux pistaches »
***
*Ambassade d'Egypte
Paris, le mercredi 23 Septembre 2009*

BELOW *An Egyptian-style figurine in the great room*
comes from the residence's collection of eighteenth-
century Sèvres biscuit.
FACING PAGE *View of the great room from the petit salon.*
The ornaments on the Corinthian pilasters, the triton,
and the garlands of flowers complete a late eighteenth-
century decor immensely appreciated in the Belle Époque.
In the present day, the drawing rooms are used for signing
agreements, for cocktail parties, and for iftars, the meal
that brings to a close the fasting month of Ramadan.

BELOW *The great room shows to their best advantage various items of furniture that were installed when the first ambassador took his post: a late nineteenth-century Sèvres vase, a painted canvas French Regency style folding-screen, a modern Egyptian stole, an armchair in the Louis XV style.*
FACING PAGE *At teatime: some delicious Om Ali ("Mother of Ali"), traditional shortcake biscuits accompanied by mint tea or by carcadé, a refreshing drink based on hibiscus flower.*

FACING PAGE *On the first floor, a painted wood staircase with a loggia landing leads to the floor housing the private apartments.*
BELOW *Serving as the ambassador's private office, the library of King Farouk on the first floor preserves its original plain wood panel decor.*

HÔTEL
PILLET-WILL

RESIDENCE OF THE AMBASSADOR
OF JAPAN

HÔTEL
PILLET-WILL

RESIDENCE OF THE AMBASSADOR
OF JAPAN

Dates of construction

1887

A private mansion is built for Count Frédéric Pillet-Will, a director of the Bank of France.
Architect Octave Raquin

1967–70

The Embassy of Japan obtains approval to construct a contemporary residence on the initial site, leaving intact only the range giving on the street.
Architect Jacques-Henri Riedberger

TO BE CONSIDERED A SUCCESS, THAT PREEMINENTLY SUBTLE ART OF JAPANESE flower arrangement called *ikebana* must astonish, render speechless even: when one enters a house and comes across a carefully composed bouquet placed in an alcove, its harmony must be such as to take one's breath away.

When, for the first time, the visitor passes through the gateway on rue de Faubourg Saint-Honoré behind which resides the Japanese ambassador to France, one is gripped by much the same sensation. From the street, one sees little more than a perfectly classical entrance with a double door resembling the majority of buildings in this up-market quarter and ones imagines that behind it lies a courtyard bordered by some noble building of a similar pedigree.

And, until 1967, one would have been right: until then there rose a residence built in 1887 by Comte Frédéric Pillet-Will, a director of the Bank of France. Today, however, nothing remains of it, save for the range giving on the street. In its place rises a modern structure of glass and aluminum whose pure lines evoke the geometry of a Zen garden.

The government of Japan acquired the Hôtel Pillet-Will in 1965, intending to turn it into a residence for its ambassador. Its interior arrangement, however, was entirely at odds with such a function and it was decided to refit it from top to bottom. As the construction stood on a site protected by the Historic Buildings Commission, the City of Paris had to set up an extraordinary planning committee. Once it was conceded that the interior could be entirely upgraded, the committee was faced with two solutions: either both frontages (to court and garden) would be preserved; or the buildings would be replaced by a modern construction by a great architect. It was the contemporary vision that was adopted.

The ambassador of Japan and his team, notably the architect Junzo Sakakura, then called upon two world-famous talents whose works were in keeping with the Japanese aesthetic: architect Jean Prouvé and designer Charlotte Perriand. The latter, in particular, was an old friend of the client country: since her first stay in 1940, she had been a frequent visitor and had resided in the country for two years in 1953–54. Finding a wealth of inspiration in Japanese art, she had moreover already been regularly collaborating with Jean Prouvé since 1939. A specialist in metallic construction, furniture-maker, and creator of architectural monuments such as the CNIT and the Tour Nobel at La Défense, in Paris, both Prouvé's frontages deploy extruded aluminum in an example of his concept of the "curtain wall" that he had been developing since 1938. In addition to its intrinsic beauty, this approach provides for an extremely luminous interior space that opens directly to the gorgeous garden. The metal-and-glass courtyard front is fitted with a wooden curtain-cum-blind screening off the interior.

PAGE 270 *The steps lead to a vast space that extends into the garden and that can be adjusted by sliding partitions depending on the number of guests. Created by Charlotte Perriand (1903–1999) and Jean Prouvé (1901–1984), these interior partitions—composed of wooden slats slotted into a slender metal armature—separate the hall from the rooms looking over the park. In the center of the hall of honor stands a polished bronze sculpture by Atsuhi Imoto entitled* Departure to Fiction.
FACING PAGE *Detail of the hall of honor, paved in white marble. This area now serves as a guest reception area: a bench-table is fitted into the marble floor. It features another piece by Atsuhi Imoto, the bronze* Birds and Keys, *and a vase by ceramist Yasokichi Tokuda.*
FOLLOWING PAGES *The entrance hall seen from the reception rooms: the main staircase consisting in white marble over an aluminum framework connects the ground floor to the first in the manner of a duplex. To the right of the staircase, the glass and metal portico. An enameled terracotta composition (1968) by painter Isao Domoto is affixed to the wall on the half-landing. Along the glazed façade to the courtyard, designer Charlotte Perriand placed a 9-meter "veil of wood slats" inspired by the palisades in similar materials that used to divide off houses from the street in Japan.*

BELOW LEFT *In the great room on the ground floor: a detail of the screen comprised of jointed blocks of fir by Perriand.*
BELOW RIGHT *Detail of the furniture in the great room created by Perriand: sections of the top of a round table in cane.*
FACING PAGE *The main room on the ground floor showing the furniture and "ambient" lighting especially designed for the residence in 1967 by Charlotte Perriand. This includes a long couch for twelve and, on the ceiling, the two electricity supply tubes fitted with adjustable lighting systems in sheet metal was an entirely new departure for the time.*

The light-filled space within was designed by Charlotte Perriand in accordance with Le Corbusier's "Modulor" rule. Thus the immense volumes of the reception space on the ground floor—broken here or there only by a partition in white metal emblazoned with the ideogram for peace or a folding-screen adorned with a cherry-tree—are preeminently harmonious. It boasts three major works by Charlotte Perriand, the sleek lines of a couch in "glulam", an articulated screen in fir wood, and an ample cane coffee table. The space is also punctuated by contemporary sculpture, while the walls are lined with modern calligraphies and prints. Through the transparent frontage, the whole opens onto the garden, a long, manicured lawn bordered by rare species of trees, some from Japan, others from France, such as an apple from Moselle that has been grafted in such a manner as to give five different varieties of fruit.

On the floor above, reached up a majestic stair that winds through the empty space, the less public rooms are cordoned off by large sliding doors: a hall where there stands a black grand piano encrusted with a gilded chrysanthemum motif, a small room furnished in Japanese traditional style giving on the court, then, in a different register, a large room filled with an art deco-inspired set of armchairs, sofas, and table-lamps; and, finally, a dining room where the garden entered by the glass front is reflected in a mirrored partition. Here, up to twenty-six diners can sit at the extendable exotic wood table decorated with a striped pattern. The Japanese chef prepares a national cuisine sometimes inflected by French influences, as testified in a recent menu which comprised, in addition to the traditional *sushis*, *sashimis,* and *miso*, roasted sea-bream topped with a sea-urchin sauce, crab and mushroom salad, and beef fillet with sesame sauce, all followed by strawberry and soya-bean millefeuille.

Every year several thousand visitors pass through the hallowed portals of this temple of light and modernity, with nearly a thousand alone for the Emperor's Birthday on December 23. Other receptions take place on the occasion of award ceremonies, fashion parades, Japanese product presentations, or to promote various regions of the archipelago.

Then there are the innumerable working lunches and dinners to which important figures from the political or economic worlds are invited. And yet, always, an ancestral proverb coming from the tea ceremony remains uppermost in the minds of the ambassador, his wife, and his inner circle alike: "Every meeting is unique." ❖

FACING PAGE, TOP LEFT AND RIGHT *Furniture in the spacious great room on the first floor: a dresser with details of its bronze fittings.*
FACING PAGE, BOTTOM LEFT *Detail of the bronze and copper handles on a chest.*
FACING PAGE, BOTTOM RIGHT *Detail in the great room: the chest from a Western-style set of furniture created by Japanese craftsmen for the country's first embassy in Paris.*
RIGHT AND BELOW RIGHT *On the first floor, a Steinway piano encrusted with copper chrysanthemums, part of a suite of Meiji furniture. In the background, the wooden strips of Perriand's "veil" screens the glass walls on aluminum crosspieces installed by the engineer Jean Prouvé.*

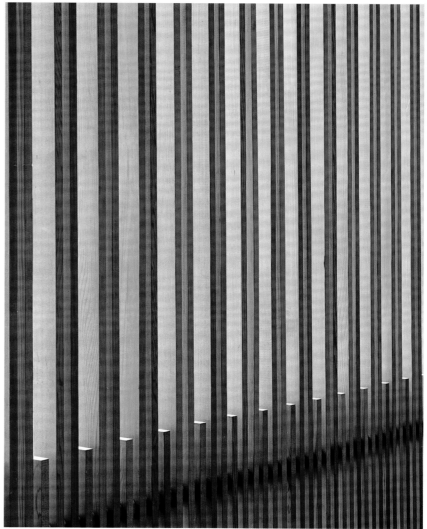

BELOW *A nishikiori, an autumn cake made from white azukis and kanten, set on a porcelain dish struck with the national emblem.*
FACING PAGE *Court side. Detail of the salon containing one of the earliest suites of furniture of Western inspiration, inlaid with copper chrysanthemums. A symbol of Japan's reforms and of her opening up to the West, it was made during the reign of Mutsuhito, the emperor who inaugurated the Meiji era in 1868.*

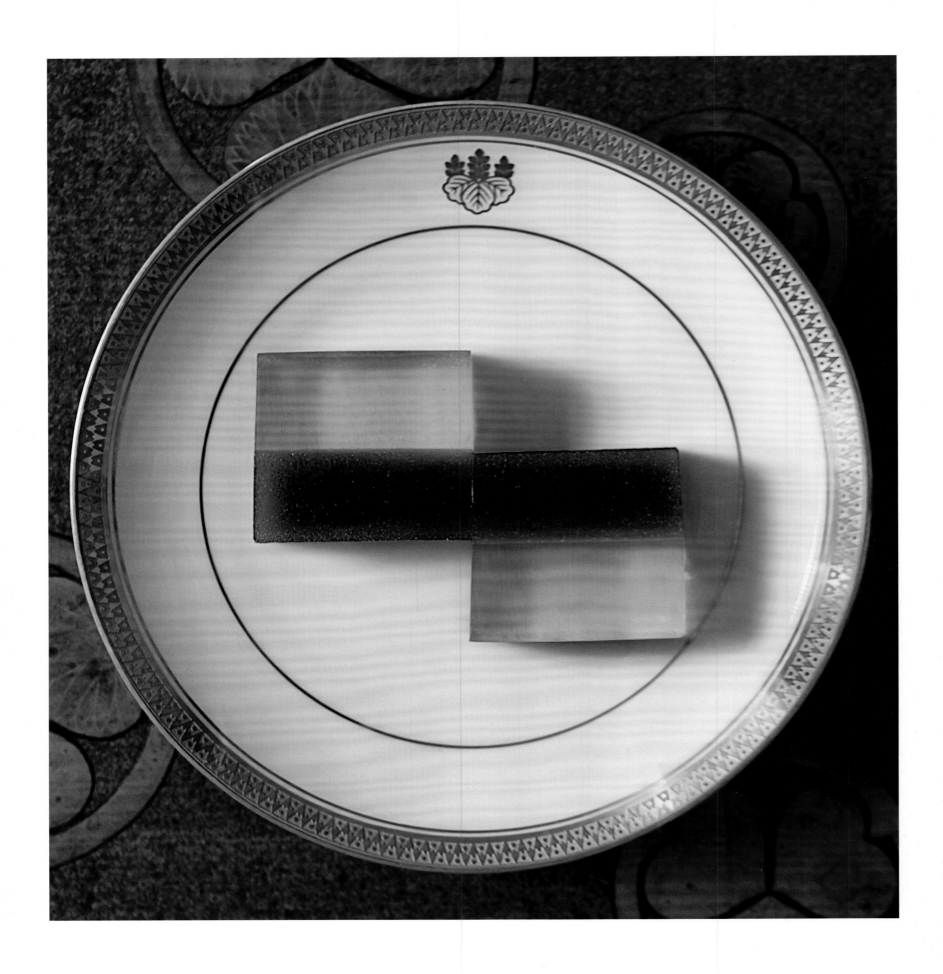

FACING PAGE *The official dining room on the first floor that looks down into the garden. The table running along the picture window is laid according to a combination of Japanese and French protocol. The lacquer tray remains in place throughout the meal for the various dishes and condiments served.*
RIGHT *Detail of the official dining room: a stoneware vase by Izuru Yamamoto.*
BELOW *A dish composed by the residence's private chef.*

HÔTEL DE ROUVRE

·

HÔTEL DE ROUVRE

CHANCELLERY OF THE EMBASSY OF THE PEOPLE'S REPUBLIC OF CHINA

Date of construction 1893

Architect Alfred Coulomb

IN 1937, THE GOVERNMENT OF KUOMINTANG WAS LOOKING FOR A RESIDENCE IN Paris worthy of housing its diplomatic mission. It soon rented a splendid private mansion erected in 1895 at the end of the avenue d'Alma (now called avenue George V) belonging to the Rouvre family of wealthy sugar producers. Ten years later, the Chinese State seized the opportunity to purchase the property outright.

On January 27, 1964, France became the first major Western country to recognize the People's Republic of China. On avenue George V, the gorgeous building became the chancellery and welcomed the country's first ambassador. The following year it was restored and its interior acquired the decor visitors see today.

After the grand staircase, one enters an entrance hall that presents a mix of traditional Chinese and historical Western architecture resembling the Shanghai of a bygone age when, in places, the two civilizations cohabited.

The eye is attracted to various Chinese works of art from Beijing and other cities, among them are two impressive reproductions of the terra-cotta warriors from the tomb of the first emperor of Qing, as well as a faithful reconstruction in reduced size of an imperial carriage, and three folding-screens embroidered on both sides with a graceful design of cats, birds, and butterflies.

In the great giltwood function room, large modern Chinese armchairs are placed for the convenience of official guests. On the mantelpiece stand the residence's two most valuable ornaments, a pair of delicate antique porcelain vases. Another very fine Qing dynasty vase can be found placed on a precious wooden sideboard in the small salon: with restrained lines and with no pattern whatsoever, this highly modern piece was designed for the emperor as a homage to the heavens. In the same room one may also admire an early twentieth-century bronze rhinoceros grazing placidly on the mantelpiece.

But the most important place in the building, one where diplomatic hospitality reaches a peak, is of course the dining room, that time-honored focus of Chinese hospitality where one of the greatest treasures of the country's civilization can be enjoyed: its gastronomy. Traditional red paper lanterns and a vast tapestry representing the Great Wall of China stand out against the paneling.

On the occasion of two major yearly events people gather here in their hundreds: the national holiday, on October 1, and the Chinese New Year, on a variable date sometime between January 21 and February 20, according to the Chinese calendar.

Official dinners are served almost every day on the small round tables in the dining room, when guests may include important figures from France, China, and other nations. The guest of honor, the head of an official delegation or the most senior of those at the table at less formal get-togethers, is always placed to the right of the ambassador.

PAGE 284 *Beneath the porch, in keeping with a custom more than a thousand years old, visitors to the ambassador and his wife are greeted by traditional red lanterns—symbols of joy and happiness.*
FACING PAGE *The main hall, framed by two lions, the guardians of the residence, leads to the reception rooms upstairs. At the foot of the staircase, a "double happiness" screen inlaid with semi-precious stones and jade.*

The chef de cuisine, as one may have suspected, is Chinese, and does his utmost to prepare the best of a thousand-year-old gastronomic tradition for the ambassador's guests. He keeps in mind some ancient basic principles, such as the balance between Yin and Yang, both for the menus and for the presentation of the various dishes. He has, however, become perfectly adapted to French ways: the entrées, for example, in addition to the inevitable soup, often comprise a cold dish such as a salad, and some recipes are not as spicy as they might be. Chinese cuisine has always been very concerned with diet and with physical wellbeing generally. So the chef may like to add to his soups medicinal plants like ginseng, or other health-giving products such as jujube, sea cucumber, and abalone.

Certain alcoholic beverages considered beneficial for the constitution, like rice wine, drunk warm and in moderation, are proposed to diners, as well as French wines, and even Chinese varieties vinified in the French manner. Official Chinese porcelain, marked with the emblem of the People's Republic, is accompanied by an impressive battery of earthenware crockery—including the highly reputed Yixing—in particular for serving individual dishes that are prepared, simmered, and served in one and the same container.

Among these delights let us quote the exceptional Fo Tiao Qiang, "the monk who jumps over the wall" (the wall that stood between him and a banquet serving this wonderfully scented dish!): a kind of slow-cooked ragout featuring ox tendron, scallops, mushrooms, quails' eggs, abalones, *yudu* (dried swim-bladder), and shark-fin. Immensely popular among the ambassador's guests, this delicious dish little known in France is served in small earthenware terrines with a lid in the shape of a monk's head. ❖

BELOW LEFT *A decorative hors-d'œuvre of tofu.*
BELOW RIGHT Yin-yang *rice soup as eaten*
at the end of a traditional meal.
FACING PAGE *In the smaller dining room a table*
laid in a combination of the Chinese
and French manners.

ABOVE *Detail of the small dining room.*
"The harmonious encounter between the crane
and the phoenix" is a dish inherited from imperial
China, the crane symbolizing long life and
the phoenix, the empress.
FACING PAGE *Detail of the "harmonious encounter*
between the crane and the phoenix," created
by one of the chefs of the residence.

FACING PAGE *Detail of the smaller dining-room:*
a 1920s cloisonné vase.
BELOW *Detail of the dining room: Yixing-clay covered*
bowls for a delicacy known as "Fo Tiao Qiang":
literally "Monk jumps over the wall."
PAGE 296 *The Green Room overlooking avenue Georges V.*
PAGE 297 *Detail of the Green Room: The Arrival of Spring,*
a calligraphy piece dating from 1964,
echoes the arrangement of chrysanthemums
by the gardener of the residence.

BELOW *The larger salon, with its reinstalled eighteenth-century gilt wainscoting, hosts a number of official receptions, including Chinese New Year. On the mantelpiece stand two Chinese blue-and-white porcelain vases.*
FACING PAGE *Detail of the larger salon: one of the blue-and-white porcelain vases with lotus flowers.*
PAGE 300 *A contemporary silk-embroidered triptych in the vestibule on the first-floor landing.*
PAGE 301 *View of the Green Room from the landing, showing an openwork wooden console on which scrolls can be unrolled and read, together with the pure contours of a ceramic vase.*

HÔTEL
D'OROSDI

RESIDENCE OF THE AMBASSADOR
OF THE REPUBLIC OF ARGENTINA

HÔTEL D'OROSDI

RESIDENCE OF THE AMBASSADOR OF THE REPUBLIC OF ARGENTINA

Date of construction 1895
Architect Jacques Hermant

PAGE 302 *The entrance porch of the embassy seen from the interior courtyard.*
BELOW LEFT *The main staircase of the embassy.*
BELOW RIGHT *A stateroom at the embassy designed during the Belle Époque.*
FACING PAGE *The vestibule at the entrance of the residence. The walls are lined with works by Argentine artists—both nineteenth century, such as Cándido López and Prilidiamo Pueyrredón, and twentieth century, like Manuel Musto and Pérez Celis—lent by the Museo Nacional des Bellas Artes in Buenos Aires. On the left, through to the dining room, the iridescent blues of La Pampa, an oil painting by Josefina Robirosa (born in 1932), once exhibited in the station "Argentine" on the Parisian Métro.*

AMBASSADORIAL RESIDENCES ARRANGED IN AN APARTMENT OFFER VISITORS a pleasing note of familial intimacy that echoing halls in large private mansions, though often of historical significance, tend to lack. This is the case with the residence of the Argentine ambassador to Paris, situated on the fourth floor of an imposing Haussmannian building in the sixteenth arrondissement. All the light from the broadest avenue in the capital floods in through the windows of a huge reception hall, decorated with marble columns with gilded Ionic capitals. A grand piano gives a clue to one of the purposes to which the room is put: musical gatherings, including regular events involving between fifty and eighty people.

The ambassador is a major collector of the kinds of accessories, generally in silver, that the gauchos wear on special occasions. Absolutely unique, these masterpieces of silverwork lie scattered on the furniture about the room: richly decorated saddles called *aperos*, stirrups, spurs, belt buckles, and daggers, not to mention an exceptional collection of *mate* bottles, for that traditional infusion that keeps the gauchos on the move (with the finely ornamented silver *bombilla*, or filtering straw), in a showcase. Among these remarkable objects, the ambassador and his wife have placed works of art with connections to world of the *pampa*, including pictures and a series of small bronzes figuring horses or bulls.

To the other side of the entrance, marble patterned walls and an inswept picture window sheltering a garden of houseplants make a fine-looking setting for the dining room with a table able to seat up to twenty guests for lunches and dinners.

The French chef has learned about Argentine gastronomy and particularly about its beef, probably the best in the world and surely the most tender . . . given that it can be eaten, even just grilled, without using a knife! The chef is now no less familiar with *empanadas*, another great specialty. All these delicacies, which go wonderfully with a cuisine of a more decidedly French tenor, are accompanied by Argentine wines. The service is of French porcelain, bordered by gold edging on a silvery blue ground: the Argentine national color.

LEFT *Detail of the decor in the entrance hall. Some calabacillas: engraved silver mate gourds with straws for filtering the tea, masterpieces of silverwork dating from the eighteenth and nineteenth centuries from the personal collection of the ambassador and his wife. Nowadays, mate, also sometimes known as Paraguayan tea or Jesuit tea—from the plantations established by Jesuit missions upstream on the Rio Parana in the colonial era in the seventeenth century—remains the national drink of Argentina.*

BELOW LEFT *A couple of empanadas ají, a cumin-flavored pastry stuffed with beef concocted by the residence's French chef.*

BELOW RIGHT *A dish of beef asado—that is, sealed over burning embers, as traditional among the gauchos of the Pampa and accompanied by a spicy sauce, salsa criolla.*

FACING PAGE *Boleadoras, the gaucho's throwing weapons used to hobble the wild horses of the Pampa; collector's items from the nineteenth century in ivory and silver arranged on another accessory no less essential to gaucho life: a faja, a woven sash worn beneath a braided rawhide belt in which he sticks a facon, a long-bladed knife whose uses are numerous.*

All the rooms of the apartment that can be visited are decorated with paintings by artists from the homeland, from all periods and in all styles, lent by the Fine Art Museum in Buenos Aires. Particularly remarkable are canvases by the great landscape painters and portraitists Prilidiano Pueyrredón (1823–1870) and Eduardo Sivori (1847–1918), as well as a Dufy-like landscape typical of the manner of the much-vaunted Josefina Robirosa (born 1932).

A few hundred meters away, at 6 rue Cimarosa, the Argentine embassy is housed in the Hôtel d'Orosdi, a turn-of-the-century building erected in 1895 by the architect Jacques Hermant for the wealthy businessman and inveterate collector Léon Orosdi, who was also Turkish consul-general in Lyon. By his death in 1923, the mansion had become a veritable museum of modern art, boasting paintings by Sisley, Degas, Fantin-Latour, Toulouse-Lautrec, and so on, all promptly sold off at auction. The building was bought in 1926 by the Republic of Argentina for its embassy. It was completely restored in 2009.

A magnificent set of nineteenth-century furniture with ivory inlays is of particular interest. On the storey below, the dazzlingly exotic Moresque Room today serves as the library. In front of rows of books, the shelves are lined with photographs of some of Argentina's foremost authors including Julio Cortazar, Ernesto Sábato, Adolfo Bioy Casares, and Silvina Ocampo.

The building also houses a huge hall of honor for more official receptions (it can also cater for far more guests than the private residence), in particular for the national holiday on May 25. ❖

RIGHT *Decorative objects from the nineteenth century reflecting the grand Argentinean silversmith's tradition.*
BELOW LEFT *Detail in the great room: some of the chef's alfajores, Argentine corn starch macaroons stuffed with dulce de leche standing on a nineteenth-century faïence dish.*
BELOW RIGHT *Detail of the table laid with the residence's fine official porcelain.*
FACING PAGE *The table set for a formal dinner in the dining room lined with Italian marble and adorned with pilasters and carved overdoors.*

HÔTEL
DE LOTA

•

RESIDENCE OF THE AMBASSADOR
OF THE REPUBLIC OF CÔTE D'IVOIRE

HÔTEL DE LOTA

RESIDENCE OF THE AMBASSADOR OF THE REPUBLIC OF CÔTE D'IVOIRE

Date of construction 1905

Architect Charles Stoullig

WHEN THEY RECEIVE GUESTS FROM THE HOMELAND, AND EVEN SOMETIMES FROM France, the ambassador of Côte d'Ivoire and his wife proceed with the same rites of hospitality in their residence on rue de Lota in the sixteenth arrondissement as they would in Africa. Such ancestral ceremonies seem immune to modernity: first the visitor is offered a glass of water and then he is asked what other drink he would like; then he is asked for news about his family and health. Once these preambles are over, enquiries are made as to the motif of his visit and business begins in earnest.

This immutable ritual possesses a well-defined function that is perfectly adapted to a diplomatic residence: the aim is to calm the waters between the outsider and the family at a time when the slightest misunderstanding could easily sour relations.

Purchased by the state of Côte d'Ivoire in 1967, this mid-nineteenth century Parisian mansion is thus filled with easy-going African customs: not only the exuberant colors of the life of that continent, the warmth, generosity, and unaffectedness of the personnel, the refinement of a traditional interior, but also the unusual but delicious flavors of a cuisine that feels drenched in sunlight.

The ambassadress has made a point of adding decorative touches from her homeland to an interior that appeared rather impersonal and "international." At the entrance one cannot help but notice several fine examples of wood carving: a splendid period traveler's trunk, a set of carved chairs ornamented in gold, and a lamp mounted on an old window from a Senufo house.

The staircase linking the five floors of the building is dotted about with traditional stools and pictures. The great hall on the first storey is decorated with contemporary works signed by famous artists, such as the French abstract painter and architect Jean-Claude Heinen or Monné Bou from Côte d'Ivoire.

But the art of living and of receiving characteristic of the homeland is best illustrated at a table where one can savor a traditional cuisine rich in exotic ingredients, fortunately readily available in Paris.

On fine days, such convivial moments can be enjoyed on the residence's roof terrace, recently revamped to serve as a venue for receptions. Here, the exotic wooden floor, the tables, the carved seats, the whipped cane on the armchairs, and, especially, the exotically luxuriant ornamental plants, create an African haven high up among the roofs of Paris.

PAGE 316 *Beneath the vault of the main staircase, traditional furniture from Côte d'Ivoire in iroko wood, carved with geometrical motifs and encrusted with gold.*

PAGE 317 *A table for a guest is laid on a woven cloth from the center of the country: the spoon made out of a calabash, while the plate and spice bottle in clay contain powdered shrimp, gumbos (lady's fingers), and peppers or pili pili.*

TOP RIGHT *A selection of gumbos and baby eggplants, essential ingredients in many sauces.*

BOTTOM LEFT *The preparation of plakali, a manioc paste with added plantain banana, an ever-present ingredient in the daily meal. The cloth here comes from the central region.*

BOTTOM RIGHT *Some attiéké, manioc semolina served on porcelain marked with the national emblem. Attiéké is a fine accompaniment with forest game, grilled snails, river or lagoon fish, as well as with seafood.*

BELOW *The motifs and colors on these textiles give clues as to the region in which they were woven.*

FACING PAGE *Ceremonial wrap, gold ornaments, jewelry, and insignia worn by a traditional Agni king in the southeast of the country. Settling in Côte d'Ivoire in the eighteenth century, the Agni ethnic group is well known for its venerable goldworking tradition.*

At table, as well as a porcelain service stamped with the emblem of Côte d'Ivoire—an elephant's head flanked by two palm-trees—the setting also features the full range of traditional utensils and containers: little calabashes serve as spoons for rice, corn, millet, or sorghum porridge; clay bowls contain sauces; wooden tumblers for water or a palm wine called *bangui*; vessels for salt and pepper made of clay; and even a splendid wine or champagne bucket, also in clay, decorated with a carved head. The plates are placed on coasters made of rare *bete* wood embellished with gold weights from Baoule country. This glorious service is laid out on resplendent traditional fabrics that act as tablecloths: wide scarves and other textiles adorned with traditional brightly colored geometrical motifs.

For major receptions, the maître d'hôtel can appear bedecked in full ceremonial costume, with a black band dripping with gold pendants tied around his forehead. The dishes he presents are all prepared by the residence's chef, who hails from the homeland. If the guests come from various countries, such local preparations are always served in conjunction with a French dish. Côte d'Ivoire cooking is enjoyed by all the guests, as long as the sauce is not made too spicy. If all the guests are from back home, the habit of serving men first is respected. French visitors, however, discover a subtle, little-known cuisine: fried sweet plantains accompanied by a pepper puree as a cocktail snack, then entrées such as *attieké à la bassamoise* (manioc couscous with fish and vegetables) or banana *akpessi* (containing plantain, smoked fish, and vegetables). Main dishes might be, for example, free-range chicken *kedjenou*—that is to say, a splendid bird, steamed with vegetables and hot peppers, served with manioc or rice couscous.

A number of French wines go well with these rather punchy dishes, as does *bangui*, and even, in moderation, *koutoukou*, a reinvigorating alcohol distilled from the palm. Thus, in Paris, can one savor, and in a manner inevitably more convivial than at the embassy, both the hospitality and the diplomacy of Côte d'Ivoire. ❧

HÔTEL DE LA
TOUR D'AUVERGNE

RESIDENCE OF THE AMBASSADOR
OF THE REPUBLIC OF CHILE

HÔTEL DE LA TOUR D'AUVERGNE

RESIDENCE OF THE AMBASSADOR OF THE REPUBLIC OF CHILE

Date of construction 1907
Architect René Sergent

IT IS OCTOBER 21, 1971: THE CHILEAN AMBASSADOR TO FRANCE IS IN HIS RESIDENCE on avenue de la Motte-Picquet, more exactly in the Chinese Room which lies next to the library, when he learns he has just been awarded the Nobel Prize for Literature. This exceptional diplomat and great writer is none other than Pablo Neruda, named as his country's representative in Paris by President Allende. At this time, the residence was a hotbed of artistic and intellectual ferment that reflected the fame and political commitment of the poet: actors Yves Montand and Simone Signoret, writer Louis Aragon, and many other iconic figures of the French Left were close friends.

Today, the La Tour d'Auvergne residence is no less buzzing: the time-honored tradition of friendship between Chile and France has been compounded in recent years by the economic dynamism of the "jaguar" of South America.

The building was erected from 1907 on by the architect René Sergent, eminent creator of residences and châteaus such as the Hôtel de Marlborough, the current residence of the Indian ambassador to Paris. It had been commissioned by Prince Henri de La Tour d'Auvergne-Lauragais, whose wife, Elisabeth, born Princesse de Wagram, grandniece of Empress Elisabeth of Austria and King Ludwig II of Bavaria, was one of the great luminaries of Belle Époque Paris.

The majestically classical decor of the building René Sergent designed for the couple is illustrated on entering by the impressive main staircase with a wrought-iron banister crowned by a gallery with a colonnade and lit by a domed skylight. To embellish the reception floor, the Prince de La Tour d'Auvergne bought three ensembles of wood-paneling from the Hôtel d'Aumont situated place Louis XV (now the place de la Concorde) and erected at the end of the 1770s which the Crillon family had recently sold to the department stores and residences firm of the Louvre which transformed the building into the palace one sees today.

Adapted to its new volumes, the famous eighteenth-century paneling now adorns several rooms, the formal dining room—where four niches contain large stucco statues and an impressive Baccarat crystal chandelier hangs over a great, thirty-two cover table—and a small rotunda-shaped salon. The floor above also incorporates a gorgeous wood-lined library holding many volumes of contemporary Chilean literature—including of course the works of Pablo Neruda—as well as more institutional works on the history or constitution of the homeland. The Chinese Salon is adorned with four large-sized panels painted on canvas in the *chinoiserie* style then in vogue.

PAGE 320 *The hall of honor, flanked with two marble statues that once belonged to the prince de La Tour d'Auvergne, who built the residence now bearing his name.*
FACING PAGE *Lit by elaborate skylights and graced with a colonnaded loggia, the main staircase leads to the reception rooms on the first floor. It is the work of a late-nineteenth-century architect who was a keen adherent of the classical style of the eighteenth.*

Shortly after the First World War, preferring the calm of the Château de Grosbois to their *hôtel*, the La Tour d'Auvergne family initially rented out the Parisian residence to the United States ambassador, before selling it to the Chilean State, together with the furniture, in 1929.

Eight decades later, the impression that time has stood still would be overwhelming indeed were it not that the residence is also the venue for a steady stream of eminently contemporary events, such as the promotion of a Chilean artist (sometimes a Parisian resident), or a writer on the launch of a French translation, or a musician at a classical music concert.

The residence, however, remains first and foremost a place for diplomatic and economic meetings. The upsurge in the Chilean economy has proved a magnet to many industrialists, who are often briefed at working breakfasts or lunches or invited to cocktail parties and dinners. In addition, the dual function of the ambassador, who is also Chile's representative at UNESCO, means there is no lack of opportunity to meet with diplomats.

The residence does not employ a full-time professional cook: for everyday meals or small get-togethers, the two maîtres d' and two chambermaids prepare traditional Chilean cuisine, in general accompanied by Chilean wines: the table is then often graced with the traditional *ceviche* (marinated raw fish), *pastel de choclo* (a gratin with maize served in little terrines), or meat or cheese *empanadas*, not forgetting *pan amasado*, a small, round homemade cornbread, nor of course, as an aperitif, the inevitable *pisco sour* (a specialty shared with Peru).

A chef is specially taken on though for larger functions, such as, for example, a visit by the President. For these events, seven or eight small tables are set up in the Salon Chinois. As in all Chilean diplomatic residences, the service is in German porcelain emblazoned with the nation's escutcheon, the cutlery Christofle (the purely classical Spatours model), while the glassware comes from a Chilean manufacture. The ghost of the Princesse de La Tour d'Auvergne who employed, it is said, the finest chef in Europe then seems to smile down on proceedings. ❖

LEFT *Detail of a wall panel in the dining room.*
BELOW LEFT AND RIGHT *Detail of a table set for an official function.
A menu card stamped with the national coat of arms.*
FACING PAGE *With an entire interior designed by Pierre
Adrien Pâris, the dining room has been listed as an
historic monument. King Louis XV would often turn
to this artist to devise festivals, ceremonies, and balls at
court. The statues are the work of a sculptor from Genoa,
Augustin Bocciardi. Dating from the eighteenth century,
the interior decor was taken from the hôtel belonging
to the Crillon family and reinstalled in the residence
in the early twentieth century.*
PAGE 328 *In the great room, view of the painted
and carved woodwork in the Louis XVI style on
a mirror-glass door opening onto the Salon Chinois.*
PAGE 329 *A loggia in the great room now fitted out
as a library.*

HÔTEL DE LÉVY

RESIDENCE OF THE AMBASSADOR
OF THE PORTUGUESE REPUBLIC

HÔTEL DE LÉVY

RESIDENCE OF THE AMBASSADOR OF THE PORTUGUESE REPUBLIC

Date of construction 1908
Architect Henri Parent

PAGE 330 *Detail of the hall of honor: a trompe l'œil flower basin takes its place in an eighteenth-century-style setting composed in 1908 by the architectural bureau of Henri and Louis Parent.*
BELOW LEFT AND RIGHT *Detail of wrought-iron scrolls and of the open-well staircase leading up to the library, the minister's suite, and the private apartments.*
FACING PAGE *Detail of the hall of honor: this short flight of steps conducts to the great gallery leading to the reception rooms that give onto the rue de Noisiel. Today, the gallery is used especially for multilateral diplomatic meetings, exhibitions by Portuguese artists, and evening concerts.*

WITH ITS MAJESTIC HAUSSMANNIAN FRONTAGE HALF-HIDDEN BEHIND THE GREAT trees of the garden and interrupted by a gracefully projecting rotunda, the Hôtel de Lévy is an unexpected, somewhat mysterious apparition at the corner of rue Spontini and rue de Noisiel.

We are in the heart of the sixteenth arrondissement of Paris, on land that once belonged to the Menier family of *chocolatiers*, whose residence and factory were located at Noisiel, in the department of Seine-et-Marne. Dating back to 1908, the building was the brainchild of the architectural practice of Henri and Louis Parent, who built a large number of private mansions and châteaus at the turn of the twentieth century.

It had been commissioned by Raphaël-Georges Lévy—who had recently acquired a section of the plot—a businessman, financier, economist of repute, and senator, as well as a relative of Marcel Proust's (his sister had married the first cousin to the writer's mother). He also occasionally acted as Proust's financial adviser. Raphaël-Georges Lévy occupied the house until his death in 1933. Ill and unable to go out, he spent the final years of his life entertaining artists, intellectuals, and businessmen in his reception rooms. During the First World War, he had converted the residence into a military hospital, occupying two small rooms on the floor above with his wife and financing the care of the casualties. On January 1, 1936, the Portuguese State bought the residence from his heirs with the intention of turning it into the chancellery and the ambassador's residence. The premises were unfortunately abandoned during the Second World War, when the Portuguese diplomatic services were established in Vichy.

In 1945, the ambassador returned to find the building devastated. The decision was taken to refurnish and restore it entirely, and pieces from the Portuguese State-owned furniture collection were brought in, while some splendid pieces, objets d'art and carpets, were acquired in France.

In the vestibule, visitors are greeted by a lovely floral composition in an echo of eighteenth-century trompe-l'œil showing a vase overflowing with flowers in a stone niche. A couple of steps lead to a great gallery containing the first significant treasures: the

FACING PAGE *Detail of the end of the long room:*
a Second Empire mahogany sideboard with claw
feet and gilt bronze brackets, over which hangs
a picture attributed to Dutch painter Johannes
Lingelbach (1622–1674).
BELOW *Detail of the painting by Johannes Lingelbach:*
the procession of the Infante Catherine of Braganza
setting off in 1662 to marry Charles II of England.
The cortege extends from the Royal Palace
on the Terreiro do Paço on the banks of the Tagus,
thus providing an historic view of the palace
esplanade before the earthquake of 1755
obliterated Lisbon's lower city.

floor is graced with an imposing *savonnerie* rug, while on a console stands the Sèvres cup presented by the Emperor to Cambacérès and adorned with a motif representing the wedding of Stéphanie Napoléon (niece of Joséphine de Beauharnais and adopted by the Emperor) with Charles de Bade; a vast Brussels tapestry dated 1600, and, strikingly, above a Louis XVI commode, an intriguing picture by the Dutch painter Johannes Lingelbach (1622–1674) and depicting a wedding procession taking place on the Terreio do Paço in seventeenth-century Lisbon before the fire of 1755, teeming with a thousand details of everyday urban life.

A Steinway baby grand is a reminder of the purpose of this impressively spacious gallery today: to receive the Portuguese and the friends of Portugal in huge numbers for lectures, exhibitions, or concerts, for a cocktail party or a presentation of Portuguese produce, and so on. It is also here, naturally, that more than six hundred people congregate on June 10 for the national holiday. Guests also gather in the great hall, where they can admire East India Company porcelain with a flower pattern dating from the seventeenth and eighteenth centuries arranged on sideboards.

The evocation of colonial Portugal continues in the very precious sixteenth-century Indo-Portuguese silver-thread embroidered silk bedspread that decorates the atrium at the foot of the great staircase leading to the floor above. The great salon extends into a smaller, round hall furnished with a splendid set of Louis XVI armchairs with upholstery illustrated by episodes from La Fontaine's *Fables*.

The many dinners and lunches are served in the dining room hung with a vast chandelier. The table is laid with very fine Vista Alegre porcelain marked with the blazon of Portugal in the center, accompanied by Atlantis crystal glass—one of the purest in the world—and, most notably, some resplendent silverware of Louis XV style marked "Rosas."

The room is adorned with six large panels in the eighteenth-century manner depicting the arts and sciences against a pastoral backdrop. Fitted and aligned perfectly to the walls, they were surely installed by the Lévy family when the mansion was built and thus constitute one of the rare remnants of the original decor.

BELOW *Detail of the furniture in the great gallery: an eighteenth-century Indo-Portuguese trunk—inlaid with exotic wood, encrusted with bone and ivory, and fitted with copper lockplates—is flanked by two chairs upholstered in Aubusson tapestry-work.*

FACING PAGE *Detail of the Indo-Portuguese coffer, called a contador, in which wealthy families would transport valuables. It reminds one moreover that it was Portuguese navigator Vasco da Gama who discovered the route to the Indies and that the Portuguese were already establishing a seaborne empire by the beginning of the sixteenth century. A Japanese porcelain Imari bowl, imported into Europe by the Dutch: from the seventeenth century such china was much sought-after by aristocratic Portuguese families.*

PAGE 338 *The rotunda. A detail of a trompe l'œil in oil in one of the four decorative niches showing motifs of vases, flowers, and birds, in vogue in the eighteenth century.*

PAGE 339 *View of the rotunda featuring eighteenth-century furniture upholstered with motifs from La Fontaine's Fables chosen by the Portuguese architect Raul Lino (1879–1974), who was appointed to restore the residence that had been severely damaged in the Second World War.*

Diplomats from the European Union and the former colonies, French and Portuguese artists and intellectuals, entrepreneurs, and Portuguese nationals or personalities of Portuguese descent residing in France (45,000 French firms belong either to Portuguese nationals or to the descendants of Portuguese nationals, while no fewer than 3,500 French elected officials are of Portuguese origin), can here enjoy the culinary skills of Maria, the cook: French cuisine sometimes, but more often great classic Portuguese dishes, such as cod in a thousand manifestations, or *arroz de pato* (duck with rice), *pastéis de nata* (little puff-pastry flans), and so on.

The ambassador's private apartment lies on the first floor. There, more intimate, less solemn receptions for fellow professionals, friends, or family take place. A gorgeous wood-paneled library lined with books harbors some first-rate East India Company porcelain in two large vitrines. Another, smaller room is adorned with a full-length portrait of a young woman wearing trousers, executed in the Modern Style by the painter Eduardo Malta in 1938. The private apartments also boast two canvases by the famous Vieira da Silva and her husband Arpad Szenes, who both settled in France in the 1920s and whose praises were often sung by the poet René Char. The second storey contains a dozen or so offices including the ambassador's, reminding visitors that the Hôtel de Lévy is also a working embassy open from morning to night. ❧

ABOVE *View of the great room opening into the formal dining room. In the early days of the First World War, Raphaël-Georges Lévy—a relative of Marcel Proust's and senator for the department of the Seine, who had inaugurated the construction of the mansion—opted to stay in Paris, where, assisted by his wife, he converted his sumptuous residence into a military hospital.*

FACING PAGE *Detail of the grand salon: one of four panels in wood painted on a gold ground probably from a palace in Portugal and remounted on the initiative of the architect Raul Lino, who oversaw the restoration of the residence from 1946 to 1950, a task he continued even after his appointment in 1949 as director of the national architectural heritage of Portugal.*

PRECEDING PAGES *A half-oval projecting toward the street, the formal dining room, decorated with six eighteenth-century manner pictures of pastoral scenes illustrating the arts and sciences, caters for up to twenty guests. The decor here was also revamped by Raul Lino. In the middle of the table, a silver centerpiece in the João V style made in the workshops of the Rosas family, established in Porto since 1851. On the floor, a carpet by the manufacture at Arraiolos in the province of Alentejo, a center of weaving for some four centuries.*

FACING PAGE *Detail of the table laid for an official function: in accordance with a time-honored tradition, the classic spinach cream is served in a fine porcelain service made by the manufactory at Vista Alegre in the province of Beiras, founded in 1824.*

ABOVE LEFT *Atlantis cut crystal.*

ABOVE RIGHT *A menu card emblazoned with the Portuguese emblem.*

RIGHT *Detail of the residence's collection of crystal glass carafes.*

BELOW LEFT *Detail of the minister's chamber:*
on the first floor, an eighteenth-century Portuguese
bombé chest-of-drawers, a collector's piece inlaid
with exotic woods.
BELOW RIGHT *Portrait of a woman in 1938*
by the painter Eduardo Malta (1900–1967).
FACING PAGE *High tea, as served in the rotunda:*
the little flans from Belém called pastéis de nata,
together with some queijadas, *are presented*
among articles of nineteenth-century silverware
made in Porto.

HÔTEL DE MARLBOROUGH

·

RESIDENCE OF THE AMBASSADOR
OF THE REPUBLIC OF INDIA

HÔTEL DE MARLBOROUGH

RESIDENCE OF THE AMBASSADOR OF THE REPUBLIC OF INDIA

Date of construction 1910
Architect René Sergent

EXQUISITE REFINEMENT COMBINED WITH UNDERSTATED INDIVIDUALISM: SUCH IS the overwhelming impression of the visitor upon exploring the residence of the Indian ambassador. The feeling arises initially from the immediate environment of this mansion that stands on the edge of the Champ de Mars, practically in the shadow of the Eiffel Tower, persisting in the perfection of a nostalgic, eighteenth-century-tinged architecture, and crowned by the concord, at once remarkable and harmonious, between the preeminently Indian and the classically French elements of its decor.

The Hôtel de Marlborough, at the corner of the avenue Charles-Floquet and the rue du General-Lambert, was erected in 1910 for a Belgian industrialist, Jules Steinbach, by the architect René Sergent. The latter was then an architect at the summit of his fame, who already had private residences for many of the wealthiest families of Europe and the United States to his credit, as well as deluxe hotels throughout the world, such as Claridge's in London and the Grand Hotel in Rome. The residence he built for Jules Steinbach was inspired by the neoclassical architecture of the eighteenth century, in particular by certain edifices by Claude-Nicolas Ledoux. This influence transpires in the residence's extremely elegant main front, with its Ionic columns and graceful bas-reliefs. The same taste reappears once through the entrance door, as one's eyes light on the main stairhall that springs from the vestibule.

Succeeding Jules Steinbach, a famous couple of the Roaring Twenties, Consuelo and Jacques Balsan, gave a second wind to the eighteenth-century decor, adding the old wood paneling that can be seen still today. Consuelo was then one of the richest and most beautiful women in the world. Only daughter of American railroad king William Kissam Vanderbilt, in 1895, when hardly eighteen, she had married Charles Spencer Churchill, Duke of Marlborough, from whom she separated eleven years afterward. Divorce was pronounced only in 1921, a year after she had acquired the residence that then took her name. The same year she married Jacques Balsan, heir to a textile manufacturing family and aviation pioneer.

PAGE 348 *Detail of the main vestibule designed in the Belle Époque by René Sergent (1865–1927), an architect who favored the classical eighteenth-century style. At the foot of the main staircase, one is greeted by the traditional burning oil lamp; on the half-landing stands a statue of Parvati, wife of the god Shiva and mother of Ganesh; in Hinduism, this perfect wife and mother is the paragon of womanhood.*
RIGHT *Detail of the fresco,* The Bodhisattva Padmapani, *the bearer of the lotus-flower, and the allegory of compassion painted by artist Krishna Hebbar (1911–1996) especially for the residence.*
FACING PAGE *On the first floor, the doors from the main drawing room, with its Regency period carved wood paneling, opens through to* The Bodhisattva Padmapani, *reproducing a scene inspired by the sixth-century frescoes discovered in the vast cave sanctuary at Ajanta in western India that illustrate the former existences and reincarnations of the Buddha. The eighteenth-century giltwood paneling was acquired and mounted by the house's first owner, Consuelo Vanderbilt, the ex-Duchess of Marlborough.*

e first floor:
peror" carpet,
d brocade
si (Benares)
he wall.
l of motifs
was specially
r for the Indian
models made
Persian emperor;
square inch.
om: a chased

to the stateroom

Intimates of the interwar jet-set, the couple was a mainstay of high society, shuttling between their various properties in the United States and in France. The Hôtel de Marlborough was then embellished, in addition to its splendid paneling, with a great number of works of art originating from the Vanderbilt family, including a Renoir *Baigneuse* hung in the great hall.

The Balsans resided in the United States during the Second World War, when Jacques—aged 73!—engaged in the Free French Air Force. Put up for sale shortly after the War, the building was bought by the Indian government in 1949, becoming the Paris residence of the country's ambassador.

It must have afforded quite a challenge to bring an Indian touch to this French neo-classical monument, but, thanks to the impeccable taste and decorum of the Indian decorators, the task has been carried off magnificently. Scrupulously preserving the wood boiseries and the painted decorations, they have restrained themselves to placing, here and there, a handful of masterpieces of the arts and crafts from the Subcontinent. The entrance hall, for instance, boasts a reproduction—by the painter Krishna Hebbar—of a fresco from one of the famous Ajanta Caves in the State of Maharashtra representing the lives and reincarnations of the Buddha. As for the large ground-floor dining room, it is decorated with splendid silk brocade dating to 1950 decorated with a hunting scene, whose impressive dimensions (approximately 5 by 3 meters in a single piece) required the use of a loom of exceptional size.

Further traditional silk panels ornament the small salon on the first floor, which offers a matchless view over the Champ de Mars and the Eiffel Tower. The Grand Salon features an impressive reproduction of a sixteenth-century "Emperor's" carpet. Bronze figures from Indian mythology appear here and there on the furniture, and are joined by paintings by Indian artists, one of the most famous being Jangarh Singh Shyam, who passed away in 2001.

The ambassador and his wife host many official or private functions to publicize the simultaneously traditional and modern image of today's India. For Indian Fashion Week in France, for example, nearly three hundred guests gathered in the residence.

The Indian chef serves only dishes from his country, but adapted to the palates of his guests—in other words, when necessary, not too spicy! The silverware on which these examples of one of the globe's most sophisticated cuisines is served is Indian, as is the magnificent porcelain marked with the coats-of-arms of the Republic and the handmade lace table settings. ❖

ABOVE *Detail in the main vestibule: a door panel from a temple showing the elephant-headed god Ganesh, the guardian of Hindu temples and houses.*

FACING PAGE *On the first floor. The library, with its natural wood paneling, looks onto the Champ-de-Mars. On the landing stands a bronze Bastar horse cast using the lost-wax process by tribes from the region of Bastar who in the twelfth century settled in the State of Chhattisgarh and who remain masters in the arts of bronzework.*

PAGE 356 *Partial view of the Petit Salon from the stateroom: a Benares gold and silver thread silk brocade has been fixed to a panel between the original antique-style pilasters and friezes.*

PAGE 357 *In the Petit Salon, a detail from a panel of the painted wooden folding screen: a bucolic scene from the life of the god Krishna.*

PAGE 358 *In the dining room on the ground floor, the table is set for an official dinner.*
PAGE 359 *Teatime: the teaspoon handles are embellished with coins dating from the period before the British Empire.*
BELOW *Desserts on a platter; certain delicacies are flavored with spices and covered in silver foil. In India, food is thought to possess restorative qualities for the spirit as well as for the body.*

FACING PAGE *Detail of the dining room: this brocade—a single length of silk measuring some five meters by three and woven in gold and silver thread in Varanasi— is emblazoned with motifs of men hunting gazelle, elephants, and hares. It was executed specifically for the residence in 1950 and woven on a loom specially adapted to take account of its large size.*

AUSTRALIA

RESIDENCE OF THE AMBASSADOR

COMMONWEALTH OF AUSTRALIA

PAGE 362 *Detail of the upper reaches of the frontage of the Chancellery—a concave quarter circle lined with slabs of granite that gazes down on the Seine. In 1973, the Australian architect Harry Seidler (1923–2006) erected a pair of 31-meter-high buildings resembling inverted fans: the first contains the offices of the Chancellery, the OECD and UNESCO missions, as well as the ambassador's residence on the top floor; next door are housed the apartments of the Chancellery employees.* LEFT *In the foreground, a detail of the apartment building in quartz concrete. In the background, the adjacent convex edifice containing the Chancellery.* BELOW *Detail of the splayed base supporting the embassy building cast in "rough concrete" by structural engineer Pier Luigi Nervi (1891–1979), a disciple of Bauhaus pioneer Marcel Breuer (1902–1981), with whom he had built the UNESCO headquarters in Paris in 1953; the substructure shelters a glass portico leading into the Chancellery.* FACING PAGE, TOP LEFT *Detail of the embassy's entrance hall: these Bone Coffins, painted with totemic signs in natural ocher pigment, symbolize the ceremony of the "Hollow Log" among the Aborigine communities of Arnhem Land (Northern Territory). On the left, a painted Pukumani post, employed in the burial ceremonies of the Tiwi people on the Island of Bathurst (Northern Territory).* FACING PAGE, TOP RIGHT *Detail of the hall: a contemporary piece of high-fired ceramic.* FACING PAGE, BOTTOM *Detail in the hall: Homage to Louis Barragán, an oil on canvas by painter Michael Johnson (born in 1938) that covers a stretch of the wall opposite some Aborigine ritual posts.*

RESIDENCE OF THE AMBASSADOR

COMMONWEALTH OF AUSTRALIA

Date of construction 1973–78
Architect Harry Seidler

BELOW LEFT *In the vestibule: detail of a symbolic motif of an Aborigine Bone Coffin.*
BELOW RIGHT *Detail of the entrance hall to the residence: Familiar Fields (1998), a painted glass vase by Karryne Smith.*
FACING PAGE *Detail of the reception room vaulted in smooth quartz concrete and painted white. The glass convex partition sets the space off from the vestibule. Above the grand piano stands Dusk was Falling #5, an oil painting by the contemporary Australian artist Lynne Boyd (born in 1953). The reception room is used both for diplomatic meetings and art events and can cater for up to one hundred and fifty people.*

THE AUSTRALIAN EMBASSY REPRESENTS ONE OF THE MOST UNUSUAL DIPLOMATIC residences in Paris: not only because of the distinct possibility of being served kangaroo steak at one of its tables, but more especially for the daring forms of a structure that offers unobstructed views over the Seine, the Palais de Chaillot, and the Eiffel Tower.

The aesthetic pleasure afforded when approaching the embassy from the quai Branly, the grand entrance, and the reception rooms of the ambassador that one discovers on the seventh floor are the work of a major Australian architect, Harry Seidler (1923–2006). As for so many of his countrymen at the time, Seidler's youth was spent in a period of upheaval and became a determinant influence on his artistic and intellectual background. Born to a Jewish family in Vienna, at the time of the Anschluss he managed to flee to Great Britain with his parents, choosing exile in Canada before finishing his architectural studies at Harvard. Training under two famous Bauhaus pioneers, Marcel Breuer and Walter Gropius, their influence transpires in all his work, particularly in the Australian embassy built in Paris between 1973 and 1977. He even turned to Breuer for help in its construction, as well as to the celebrated structural engineer, Pier Luigi Nervi; the two men responsible for the building of the UNESCO headquarters in Paris.

Harry Seidler's response to the many constraints of the site and function of the building was a brilliant one. The construction to be erected on the triangular plot was not allowed to block off the view of the Palais de Chaillot over the Champ de Mars. In addition, the embassy had to house offices as well as the residence. Inspired by Baroque architecture, the architect solved this dilemma with two buildings arranged as two convex and concave half-circles a dozen yards apart from one another. For the visitor, and even more so for the incumbent, the most immediately noticeable result of this idea is the splendid panoramic view of Paris's Right Bank.

Lastly, Seidler and his two advisers made wonderfully refined use of their materials, exploiting the contrast between the raw concrete load-bearing elements and the delicacy and extreme smoothness of the flooring, ceilings, and walls featuring granite flagstones, quartz concrete, and gray-tinted glass. The whole construction looks generously out over the lights of Paris.

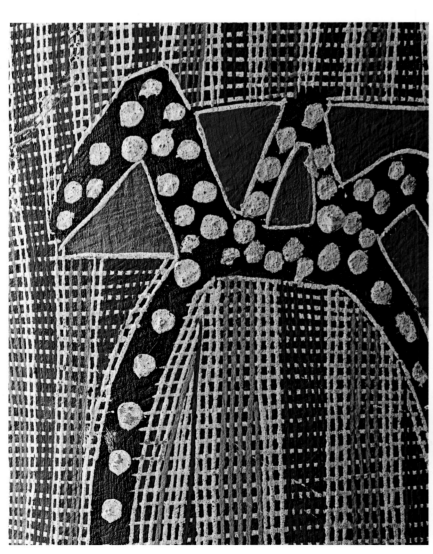

The sensuous harmony of the huge reception hall, ringed by a living room and a dining room where the ambassador and his wife receive their guests, expresses itself effortlessly in space, purity, light, and modernity. An immense picture window, prolonged by a terrace planted with blossoming magnolias, seems to embrace Paris with open arms. At night, the room is illuminated by the Eiffel Tower, scarcely more than 400 yards away. This striking effect makes an indelible impression on every guest. And, year after year, by day or night, French and Australian politicians, diplomats, artists, and intellectuals come in their droves for luncheon, dinner, or a cultural event and delight in what is a truly magical spectacle.

Some of these events are marked by full-blown functions, such as the arrival of the Australian Ballet in Paris. The size of the reception hall is if anything underscored by the room's elegant sobriety, its fitted carpet of a light color, and the scarcity of furniture—just a few armchairs and settees. A grand piano betrays the fact that musical soirées also take place here. The great hall can hold up to one hundred and fifty people.

The dining room is the venue for more intimate meals, working breakfasts or lunches, as well as for more or less official dinners. The table here is designed for a mere twenty-four covers. Each morning, the ambassador, a gourmet himself, assisted by his wife, examines the Australian chef's suggestions. His specialty is a "fusion" cuisine where Australian culinary delicacies naturally appear: in addition to the aforementioned kangaroo fillet, there may also be a sauté of lamb or salmon with asparagus. Some of the accompanying vegetables are grown in the chef's rooftop vegetable garden.

Poring over the piously conserved menus of years gone by, one relives a delicious pheasant with Lyon potatoes, prosciutto chips, and foie gras *jus*, and imagines this menu served on English porcelain adorned with the Australian coat of arms, its blazon flanked by a kangaroo and an emu. The wine list of course is not short of Australian vintages, now among the best in the world.

If the architecture evokes the essential Australian characteristics of modernity and wide-open spaces, its creators also wanted to represent the riches of the country's indigenous culture with examples of painting and sculpture. So, here and there, one comes across brightly colored labyrinths, symbolic drawings, and spiritual compositions by major Australian artists with names like Dorothy Napangardi, Anna Petyarre, Helicopter Tjungurrayi, or Joe Ngallametta. To the present and future of the largest island on the planet, they bring roots that go back tens of thousands of years. ❖

LUNCH

***

*Tuna Salmon Tartare with
Crab & Avocado Salsa and Lemon Oil*

***

*Peppered Kangaroo Fillet with
Layered Potatoes, Baby Asparagus & Beetroot Jus*

***

*Decadent Chocolate Cake with
New Season Berry Compote*

***

*Tamar Ridge Chardonnay (Tas) 2004
D'arenberg Shiraz Granache (SA) 2004*

ABOVE LEFT *Detail of a table setting: a menu card
stamped with the national insignia.*
ABOVE RIGHT *Detail of an acrylic painting on canvas by
the contemporary indigenous artist Anna Petyarre
(born in 1965), who comes from the community
of Utopia in northern Australia.*
LEFT *A chocolate fondant with fresh currant compote
as prepared by the residence's Australian chef.*
FACING PAGE *Detail of the dining room where the table
is laid for a working lunch. Above the console
table stands a picture by contemporary painter
Tommy Carroll (born in 1956), a member of the
community of Ngarrangkarni, who employs natural
vegetal pigments in his art. The door is flanked by
a pair of Thap yongk, or "Law Posts," replicas of
ritual objects from the Aurukun community, incised
and painted with clayey ocher and acrylic resin by
the Aborigine artist Joe Ngallametta (1945–2005),
from the Aurukun community.*

Bibliography

"Ambassade de Pologne, hôtel de Monaco, Paris par Piotr Witt,"
Beaux-Arts Magazine (special number), Paris, 2005.

Beal, Mary and John Cornforth, *British Embassy, Paris, the House and its Works
of Art*, (publication funded by Christie's and the Government Art Collection),
London, 1992.

De Gorter, Sadi, *L'hôtel d'Avaray, Ambassade des Pays-Bas*, The Hague:
Staatsdrukkerij (published by the embassy), 1956.

Fiechter, Jean-Jacques and Benno Schlubiger, *L'ambassade
de Suisse à Paris, hôtel de Chanac de Pompadour
ou hôtel de Bésenval*, Paris (published by the embassy), 1994.

Gady, Alexandre, *Les hôtels particuliers de Paris
du moyen-âge à la Belle Époque*, Paris: Parigramme, 2008.

Gentile Ortona, Erminia, Maria Teresa Caracciolo,
and Mario Tavella, *L'ambassade d'Italie à Paris,
hôtel de La Rochefoucauld-Doudeauville*, Paris: Skira, 2009.

Goodale, Jane, *Tiwi Wives*, Washington D.C.:
University of Washington Press, 1971.

Hamon-Jugnet, Marie and Catherine Oudin-Doglioni, *Le Quai d'Orsay,
l'hôtel du ministre des affaires étrangères*, Paris: Editions du Felin, 1991.

"L'hôtel de Béhague, la résidence de la Roumanie en France,"
Connaissance des Arts (special number), Paris, 2008.

Lazare, Félix and Louis Lazare, *Dictionnaire historique
des rues et monuments de Paris en 1855*, Paris: Maisonneuve et Larose, 2003.

Leben, Ulrich and Jörg Ebeling, "Le palais Beauharnais à Paris, un somptueux
décor Empire," *L'Objet d'Art* (special number), 400, March 2005.

Mackenzie Stuart, Amanda, *Consuelo and Alva Vanderbilt*,
New York: First Harper Perennial, 2007.

Martin de Clausonne, Elisabeth, *Les ambassades à Paris*,
Paris: Nicolas Chaudun, 2009.

Nérée Ronfort, Jean and Jean-Dominique Augarde, *A l'ombre de Pauline,
la résidence de l'ambassadeur de Grande-Bretagne à Paris*,
Paris: Editions du Centre de Recherches Historiques, 2001.

Niangoran-Bouah, *L'univers Akan des poids à peser l'or*,
Paris: Nouvelles Editions Africaines, 1984.

Paternotte de la Vaillée, Baron, *L'hôtel de la Marck, ambassade de Belgique*,
Paris: Berger-Levrault, 1982.

Perriand, Charlotte, *A Life of Creation*, New York: Monacelli, 2003.

Rousset-Charny, Gérard, *Les palais parisiens de la Belle Epoque*,
Paris: Délégation à l'Action Artistique de la Ville de Paris, 1990.

Vázquez Díaz de Tuesta, Ángel, *La Embajada de España en París*,
Madrid: Ministerio de Asuntos Exteriores, 2000.

Vega, Roberto and José M. Molína Eguíguren, *El apero críollo, arte y tradicíon*,
Buenos Aires: Editions Vega/Eguíguren, 2000.

Walker Stapleton, Dorothy, *Elegant Entertaining: Seasonal Recipes
from the American Ambassador's Residence in Paris*, Paris: Flammarion, 2009.

Acknowledgments

Bienvenue en France is pleased to join Éditions Flammarion in expressing its gratitude to the French Minister of Foreign and European Affairs, as well as to the ambassadors and their spouses, without whose commitment, cordial hospitality, and unflinching confidence this splendid volume would never have been published. Over our year's work, we came to appreciate the accessibility, patience, effectiveness, and expertise of those who, in all the many residences and chanceries, strove to provide the best conditions possible so as to make our project a reality.

ARGENTINE
H. E. Ambassador and Mrs. Luis M. URETA SAENZ PEÑA
Mrs. Consuelo de Barrigue de Fontanieu, Mr. Arnaud Belaen

AUSTRALIA
H. E. Ambassador David RITCHIE and Mrs. Irma FICARRA RITCHIE
Mrs. Chelsea Roberts, Mr. Tony Illingworth, Mr. Thierry Viguier

BELGIUM
H. E. Ambassador and Mrs. Baudouin de la KETHULLE de RYHOVE

CHILE
H. E. Ambassador Pilar ARMANET
Mr. Jaime CHOMALI, Chargé d'Affaires a.i.
Mrs. Aylin Joo
Ms. Josefina Roma, Mrs. Danièle Weinberger, Mr. Guillermo Rojel

CHINA
H. E. Ambassador Quan KONG and Mrs. Yingying WANG
Mrs. Qunhua Ying, Mrs. Yunbei Li
Mr. Lihui Zhang, Mr. Xuechun Yu, Mr. Linan Shen, Mr. Jian Wang, and Mr. Weihua Li

CÔTE D'IVOIRE
H. E. Ambassador Pierre Aimé KIPRÉ and Mrs. Colette Angélique KIPRÉ
Mrs. Khady Diallo

EGYPT
H. E. Nasser KAMEL and Mrs. Dalia EL BATAL KAMEL
Mrs. Nabila Chaieb

GERMANY
H. E. Ambassador Reinhard SCHÄFERS and Mrs. Mechthild SCHÄFERS
Mrs. Sylvia Guibert, Mrs. Farideh Afshar
Mr. Michel Isinger, Mr. Manfred Herold

INDIA
H. E. Ambassador Ranjan MATHAI and Mrs. Gita Elisabeth MATHAI

ITALY
H. E. Ambassador Giovanni CARACCIOLO DI VIETRI
Mr. Luca Laudiero, Mrs. Loreta Nocentini
Mr. Giulio Freschi, Mr. Guido Romero

JAPAN
H. E. Ambassador Yasuo SAITO and Mrs. Chieko SAITO
H. E. Ambassador Yutaka IMURA and Mrs. Haruko IMURA
Mr. Kanzo Kawaguchi

THE NETHERLANDS
H. E. Ambassador Hugo SIBLESZ
Mrs. Rozenn Bouillé
Mr. Enzo Franceschelli, Mr. Pietro Cotroneo, Mr. and Mrs. Joël Jablowski

PERU
H. E. Ambassador Harry BELEVAN-McBRIDE
and Mrs. Cecilia TAMAYO de BELEVAN
Mrs. Joseline Pozzi-Escot

POLAND
H. E. Ambassador Tomasz ORLOWSKI and Mrs. Aleksandra ORLOWSKA
Mrs. Elzbieta Burdzy, Mr. Miroslaw Nowak

PORTUGAL
H. E. Ambassador Francisco SEIXAS DA COSTA
and Mrs. Maria Virginia SEIXAS DA COSTA
Mrs. Fátima Ramos, Mr. Candido Baptista De Souza, Mrs. Maria Dulce Rita De Jesus Duarte
Mrs. Rosa Maria Lecca Solorzano

QATAR
H. E. Ambassador Mohamed Jaham AL-KUWARI
and Mrs. Aïsha AL MADEED AL-KUWARI

ROMANIA
H. E. Ambassador Teodor BACONSCHI and Mrs. Marina BACONSCHI
Mrs. Roxana IFTIMIE, Chargée d'Affaires a.i.

RUSSIA
H. E. Ambassador Alexander ORLOV and Mrs. Natalia ORLOVA
Mrs. Natalia Liubimova

SPAIN
H. E. Ambassador Francisco VILLAR Y ORTIZ DE URBINA
and Mrs. Isabel ESCUDERO BEDATE
Mrs. Maria-Antonia Cavero-Rosais, Mr. Edmondo Montalvo, Mr. Oscar Martinez Piquenque,
Mr. Pedro Blazquez Martin, Mr. Lourenço Gonçalves Sanches, Mrs. Margarita Méndez Graña

SWITZERLAND
H. E. Ambassador N. Ulrich LEHNER and Mrs. Federica LEHNER-TIMBAL
Mrs. Mariella Baserga, Mr. Christian Lesgent, Mr. Ludovic Rasschaert

THE UNITED KINGDOM
H. E. Sir Peter and Lady WESTMACOTT
Mrs. Diane Bernard, Mrs. Tess Mendibe

THE UNITED STATES
H. E. Ambassador Charles HAMMERMMAN RIVKIN and Mrs. Susan TOLSON
Mr. Daniel Dozier
Mr. Yves Roquel

THE QUAI D'ORSAY
The Ministry of Foreign and European Affairs

H. E. Mr. Bernard KOUCHNER, Minister of Foreign and European Affairs
Mr. Pierre Sellal, Secretary-General, Mr. Philippe Errera, Cabinet Director
Mr. Bachir Bakhti, Mr. Dominique Richard, Mr. Thierry Bouron
Mr. Laurent Huchet, and Mr. Abdelaziz Sahli

Thanks are also due to Mr. Richard Flahaut and Mr. Jörg Ebeling for their perspicacious eye and specialist knowledge of our heritage.

The present volume also owes its existence to Mme Catherine de Gliniasty, former president of Bienvenue en France, who first had the idea; to Dauphine de Schonen, who, together with Mme de Gliniasty, set the project in motion; to Françoise Hautcœur, through whom Bienvenue en France and the publishers Flammarion were put into contact; to Cristina Gompertz, the sitting president, who offered tireless backing to our enterprise; to Evelyn Cheuvreux, vice-president, for her judicious advice; and, last but not least, to Christine Okrent, honorary president, for her efficacious support; and to Marie-Thérèse François-Poncet, the founding president, for her unfailing encouragement.

Bienvenue en France would also like to hail our intrepid commissioning editor, Suzanne Tise-Isoré, whose talent, passion, and artistic flair meant that our initial draft was turned into this gorgeous volume.

We would like to express our thanks to the firm of Mariage Frères, who lent us some of the splendid tea articles they make.

Index

A

Adnet, Jacques 13, 23
Agni, ethnic group 318
Aguesseau, Joseph Antoine d' 176
Ahmed, Yusef 218
Ajanta, caves 350, 353
Alentejo, province of 345
Alexander III, Emperor of Russia 46, 48, 58
Alfonso XIII, King of Spain 228, 238
Allende, Salvador 322
Alma, avenue d' 228, 286
Anguisciola, Sofonisba 230
Annunzio, Gabriele d' 203
Apponyi, Anton, Count 162
Arc de Triomphe 218, 258, 314
Argentina 304, 306, 308
Arnhem Land 364
Arraiolos, carpet factory of 345
Atlantis, crystal work 335, 345
Aubusson, tapestry of 90, 118, 336
Augusta-Amelia, of Bavaria 64
Aurukun, community 370
Australia 366, 370
Austria 13, 102, 230, 322
Avaray, Claude-Théophile de
    Bésiade, Marquis d' 88
Ayvazovsky, Ivan 48

B

Baccarat, crystal works 230
Balsan, Jacques 350, 353
Balzac, Honoré de 162
Barragán, Luis 364
Bassano, Jacopo 230
Bastar, region of 354
Bastille, storming of 32
Bathurst, island of 364
Bautru de Vaubrun, Madeleine-Diane de 46
Bayard, Julien 246
Beauharnais, Eugène de 62, 64, 67, 70, 76, 81, 82
Beauharnais, Hortense de 67, 82
Beauharnais, Joséphine de, Empress of
    the French 62, 64, 67, 335
Beauvais, tapestry factory of 18, 178
Béhague, Amédée, Comtesse de 194
Béhague, Martine, de 194, 196, 203, 206, 212
Béhague, Octave, Comte de 194
Beiras, province of 345
Beistegui, Charles de 106
Belgium 144, 154
Belloni, Francesco 81
Benares 353, 354, 360
Benlliure, Mariano 238
Bérard, Christian 106
Bercy, Château de 127, 132
Bernard, Jacques Samuel 178
Bertin, Nicolas 127
Besenval, Pierre-Victor de, Baron de 32, 34, 36, 41, 43
Bésiade d'Avaray, family 88, 99
Béthune-Charost, Paul-François,
    Duc de 102
Beuvron d'Harcourt, Anne-François,
    Marquis de 46

Bidassoa, porcelain factory of 230, 237
Bienfaisance, rue de la 258
Bigot de Préameneu, Félix, Comte de 124
Bioy Casares, Adolfo 308
Bir-Hakeim, bridge 369
Biron, Louis-Antoine de Gontaut,
    Duc de 46
Bismarck, Otto von 64
Blanche, Jacques-Émile 228
Blondel, Jacques François 139
Bocciardi, Augustin 326
Boffrand, Germain 62, 64
Boisgelin, Raymond de 124
Bonaparte, Pauline, Princesse Borghese 102, 105, 106, 110, 118
Boni de Castellane, Comte 258
Borghese, Camillo, Prince 102
Borghese, Galleria 102
Borght, Gaspard van der 178
Bou, Monné 314
Boucher, François 32, 34, 92, 194, 203
Boudberg, Andrey, Baron de 46
Bouguereau, William 178
Boulogne, Bois de 46
Bourbon, Palais 170
Bourbon, rue de 62
Bourbon-Condé, Louis, Prince de 158, 170
Bourbon-Conti, Marie François Félix,
    Comte de 124
Bourbon-Salerno, Marie-Caroline de,
    Duchesse d'Aumale 18
Boyd, Lynne 366
Branly, quai 366
Breteuil, Marquise de 158
Breuer, Marcel 364, 366
Brignole-Sale, Marie-Catherine de,
    Princesse of Monaco 158, 170
Brongniart, Alexandre Théodore 32, 34, 36, 158, 162
Brunau, Félix 127
Bruneau, Pierre 13
Buenos Aires, National Museum
    of Fine Art 304, 308
Butera, Palazzo 127
BVRB, cabinetmaker (Bernard Van
    Risenburg, commonly known as) 136

C

Callias, Horace de 250, 253
Camairas, Philippe 162, 168
Cambacérès, Jean-Jacques de 335
Canada 366
Canova, Antonio 102, 106
Carroll, Tommy 370
Cars, Duc des 46
Cartaud, Jean-Sylvain 124
Castries, Charles de La Croix,
    Maréchal de 144
Catarina, de Bragança, Infanta 335
Catherine II, Empress of Russia 50
Caussin, Anne-Marie-Adèle,
    Marquise de Landolfo-Carcano 218
Celis, Pérez 304
Cervantes, Miguel de 234
Chaillot, colline de 162
Chaillot, palais de 366, 369

Champaigne, Philippe de 10
Champigneulle, Charles (Champigneulle
    fils, commonly known as) 250
Champ de Mars 350, 353, 354, 366
Champs-Élysées, avenue des 218
Chanac de Pompadour, Pierre, Abbé 32
Char, René 336
Charenton-le-Pont 132
Charles II, de Bade 335
Charles II, King of England 335
Charles III, King of Spain 237
Charles IV, King of Spain 232
Charles IX, King of France 32
Charles-Floquet, avenue 350
Charost, family 102
Chaudet, Antoine Denis 64
Chauvelin, Marquise de 144
Chhattisgarh, State of 354
Chile 322, 325
China 286, 292
Choiseul-Meuse, François Joseph de 144
Chopin, Frédéric 162, 168
Christofle, silversmiths 187, 325
Cignaroli, Vittorio Amedeo 127, 139
Cimarosa, rue 308
Clarke, Général, Duc de Feltre 46
Clignancourt, porcelain factory of 70
Clodion, Michel 32, 36
Concorde, place de la 212, 322, 325
Constantinople 48
Cooper, Sir Alfred Duff 106, 114
Cooper, Lady Diana 106
Cortázar, Julio 308
Côte d'Ivoire 314, 318
Cotte, Robert de 46
Coulomb, Alfred 286
Covadonga, Virgin of 230, 240
Coysevox, Antoine 130
Crillon, family 322, 325, 326

D

Dampt, Jean 194, 196
Dauphine, Porte 218
Davout, Maréchal 158, 162
Delacroix, Eugène 162
Delafontaine, Pierre-Maximilien 162
Delamair, Pierre Alexis 32
Delft, porcelain 95
Destailleur, Hippolyte 194
Destailleur, William 194, 206
Deux-Ponts, Duchesse de
    (Marie-Françoise-Dorothée,
    Countess Palatine of Sulzbach) 144
Didier, Jules 34
Doha 222
Domoto, Isao 272
Dubufe, Édouard 10, 13
Duncan, Isadora 212
Duvivier, Ignace-Louis 149
Duvivier, Vincent Marie Constantin 149
Dyck, Antoon Van 146

E

Edward VII, King of England 114
Egypt 62, 64, 258, 263
Eiffel, Tower 173, 246, 250, 350, 353, 366, 369

Eisenhower, Dwight David 183
Elba, island of 105
Elisabeth, Empress of Austria 322
Elizabeth II, Queen of the United
    Kingdom of Great Britain
    and Northern Ireland 110
Élysée, palace 144
England 13, 90, 335
Ephrussi, Jules 258
Estrées (de Lauzières-Thémines),
    François Annibal III, Duc d' 46
États-Unis, place des 258
Étoile, place de l' 218, 228

F

Fakhry Pacha, Mahmoud 258
Farnese, palazzo 124
Farouk I, King of Egypt 258, 263, 269
Faubourg-Saint-Germain, rue du 62, 124, 158
Faubourg-Saint-Honoré, rue du 102, 176, 272
Fauré, Gabriel 212
Fawkia, Princess 258
Fédel, Achille-Jacques 162
Flanders, tapestry of 144
Flanders, province of 88
Fo Tiao Qiang, delicacy 288, 295
Foch, avenue 258
Franklin, Benjamin 178
Frederick William III, King of Prussia 64
Frémin, René 130
French Ministry of Foreign Affairs 10
French National Assembly (Palais
    Bourbon) 170
Friends of 41, group of American
    benefactors 178
Fuad I, King of Egypt 258

G

Gabriel, avenue 106, 120
Gabriel, Palais 212
Galle, Claude 70
Gama, Vasco da 336
Garnier, Pierre Joseph 62
Gaulle, General Charles de 64, 183
Général-Lambert, rue du 350
Germany 62
Geoffroy, Georges 106
George V, avenue 228, 286, 288, 295
George VI, King of England 23
Gerhardt, Gustave-Adolphe 194, 212
Girodet-Trioson, Louis 67, 70
Gobelins, tapestry manufacture of 34, 41, 124, 127
Government Art Collection 105, 118
Goya, Francisco de 228, 232, 238, 240
Great Britain 102, 106, 258, 366
Greffulhe, Marie Riquet de Caraman-
    Chimay, Comtesse Henry 228
Grenelle, rue de 32, 48, 88, 212
Gropius, Walter 366
Grosbois, Château de 325
Gros-Caillou, quartier du 212
Guardi, Gian Antonio 127
Guérapin de Vauréal, Louis-Guy,
    archbishop of Rennes 32

H

Ha[...], Antoine 105
Ha[...]elin, rue 246
Ha[...]ilton, family of the Dukes of 118
Ha[...]court, family 46
Ha[...]smann, Georges Eugène, Baron 206
Ha[...]er, Sir George 106
He[...]bar, Krishna 350, 353
He[...]en, Jean-Claude 314
He[...]nant, Jacques 304, 308
He[...]mitage, State Museum 46, 48
He[...]sch de Janvry, Gérard 124
Hi[...]orff, Jacques Ignace 70, 74
Ho[...]oré III, of Monaco 158
Ho[...]el Berthier de Wagram 228
Ho[...]el Chanac de Pompadour (today,
    [...]ôtel de Besenval) 32
Ho[...]el d'Aumont 322
Ho[...]el d'Avaray 88
Ho[...]el d'Estrées 46, 48
Ho[...]el d'Orosdi 304, 308
Ho[...]el de Beauharnais 7, 62, 64, 67, 82
Ho[...]el de Béhague 5, 194
Ho[...]el de Besenval (formerly, Hôtel
    [...]hanac de Pompadour) 32
Ho[...]el de Biron 178
Ho[...]el de Boisgelin (today, Hôtel de La
    [...]ochefoucauld-Doudeauville) 124
Ho[...]el de Broglie 258
Ho[...]el de Charost 102
Ho[...]el de La Marck 144
Ho[...]el de La Rochefoucauld-Doudeauville
    [...]ormerly, Hôtel de Boisgelin) 124
Ho[...]el de La Tour d'Auvergne 322
Ho[...]el de Lévy 332, 336
Ho[...]el de Lota 314
Ho[...]el de Marigny 13
Ho[...]el de Marlborough 322, 350, 353
Ho[...]el de Monaco 158, 162
Ho[...]el de Noailles 258
Ho[...]el de Pontalba 176, 178
Ho[...]el de Rohan 32
Ho[...]el de Rouvre 286
Ho[...]el de Soubise 32
Ho[...]el des Maréchaux 218
Ho[...]el du Cèdre 162
Ho[...]el of the French Ministry
    of Foreign Affairs 10
Ho[...]el Ephrussi 258
Ho[...]el Lafont de La Vernède 246
Ho[...]el Landolfo-Carcano 218
Ho[...]el Pillet-Will 272
Li[...]chtenburg, Jan Van 97
Hu[...]et Jean-Baptiste 144, 150
Hu[...]et, Salon des 150

I

[...]na, avenue d' 258
[...]ari, porcelain 336
[...]noto, Atsushi 272
[...]dia 222, 322, 350, 353, 360
[...]gres, Jean-Auguste-Dominique 168
[...]valides, esplanade of the 10, 173, 176
[...]aly 62, 124, 127

J

[...]acob-Desmalter, François Honoré
    67, 82

Japan 272, 276, 279, 280
Jefferson, Thomas 176, 178, 183
Jenatsch, Georg 32
Johnson, Michael 364
Johnston, Nathaniel 228
Joséphine, avenue 228
Juan Carlos I, King of Spain 13

K

Kalkbrenner, Friedrich Wilhelm 162
Kashmir, State of 353
Kléber, avenue 246, 250
KPM, (Königliche Porzellan Manufaktur,
    commonly known as) 67, 68
Kuna, Henryk 173

L

La Fayette, Gilbert du Motier, General
    and Marquis de 144, 178
La Fontaine, Jean de 41, 48, 150,
    335, 336
La Marck, Auguste d'Arenberg,
    Comte de 102
La Marck, Louis Engelbert, Comte de
    144
La Rochefoucauld-Doudeauville,
    family, de 127
La Rochefoucauld, Louis Sosthène de,
    Duc de Doudeauville 124
La Rochefoucauld, Marie Charles
    Sosthène de, Duc de Bisaccia 124
La Suze, Marquise de 32
La Tour d'Auvergne-Lauragais, Prince
    de 322
La Tour d'Auvergne-Lauragais,
    Élisabeth, Princesse de Wagram
    and Princesse de 322
Labouret, Auguste 13, 23
Lacornée, Jacques 10
Lafont de La Vernède, family 246
Lancret, Nicolas 48, 58
Landolfo-Carcano, Anne-Marie-Adèle,
    Marquise de 218
Landolfo-Carnaco Marquis de 218
Langlais, Félix 176, 188
Lannes, boulevard 46
Le Bègue, Stéphane 228
Le Brun, Charles 34, 41, 199
Le Corbusier, (Charles-Edouard
    Jeanneret-Gris, commonly known as)
    276
Ledoux, Claude-Nicolas 350
Lefèvre, Robert 106
Lenin, Vladimir Ilitch Oulianov 46
Leroux, Jean-Baptiste 88
Lévy, family 335
Lévy, Raphaël-Georges 332, 340
Leyden, Lucas Van 10
Liénard, Michel Joseph Napoléon 10,
    14, 18
Lille, rue de 62, 176
Limoges, porcelain 18, 144, 187
Lindbergh, Charles 176, 178, 183
Lingelbach, Johannes 335
Lino da Silva, Raul 336, 340, 345
Lisbon 345
Liszt, Franz 162, 168
Llaneces, José 228

Loewi, Adolfo 127, 130, 136, 139
London 102, 124, 350
López, Cándido 304
Lorraine, Camille de, Prince de Marsan
    124
Lota, rue de 314
Loudon, family 90
Loudon, John 88
Louis XIV, King of France 34, 41, 46,
    62, 168, 178, 196
Louis XV, King of France 41, 178, 326
Louis XVI, King of France 144
Louis-Philippe, King of France 18, 118,
    168
Louis XV, place 322
Louvre, museum 32, 36, 130, 178, 322
Loven, François Joseph 106
Ludwig II, King of Bavaria 322
Lyon 82, 308

M

Madrid, royal manufacture of 230, 232,
    234
Maes, Nicolas 88, 144, 146
Maharashtra, state of 353
Maine, Duchesse du 187
Malmaison, Château de 68
Malta, Eduardo 336, 346
Mamluks, portraits of 64
Mamelouks, salon des 64, 67, 68
Mangonot, Charles 18
Marceau, avenue 228
Margaret of Austria, infanta of Spain
    230
Maria Luisa of Parma, Queen of Spain
    232
Marlborough, Charles Spencer Churchill,
    Duke of 350
Mauritshuis, museum 90
Maximilian I, King of Bavaria 64
Mazerolle, Alexis-Joseph 218
Mazin, Antoine 102
Meiji, era 279, 280
Menier, family 332
Mercy-Argenteau, Eugène, Comte de
    144
Migeon, Pierre II 228
Montholon de Semonville, family
    32
Motte-Picquet, avenue de la 322
Mubarak, Hosni 263
Musset, Alfred de 162
Musto, Manuel 304
Mutsuhito, Emperor of Japan 280

N

Napangardi, Dorothy 369
Napoléon I, Emperor of France 62, 64,
    102, 105, 106, 176, 218
Napoléon III, Emperor of France
    13, 18, 40
Napoléon, Bonaparte 62, 68, 124
Napoléon, Stéphanie
    (born de Beauharnais) 335
Neruda, Pablo 322
Nervi, Pier Luigi 364, 366
Netherlands, kingdom of the 88, 90, 95
Ngallametta, Joe 369, 370

Ngarrangkarni, community 370
Nicolas II, Tsar of Russia 48
Noisiel, rue de 332
Nolau, François 18
Notre-Dame de Paris, cathedral of
    34, 41
Nymphenburg, porcelain manufacture
    of 68
Nyon, porcelain manufacture of 32

O

Ocampo, Silvina 308
Orange, William III, Prince of 90, 97
Orléans, Charlotte Aglaé d', Duchess of
    Modena 46
Orléans, Marie d', Duchesse de
    Wurtemberg 18
Orosdi, Léon 308
Orsay, palais d' 10
Orsay, quai d' 10, 13
Orsay, the Quai d' 10, 13
Oudry, Jean-Baptiste 162

P

Paillard, Victor 14
Palais Rose 258
Palermo, palace of 127
Pantoja de la Cruz, Juan 230
Paraná, river 306
Parent, Henri 124, 127, 332
Parent, Louis 332
Pâris, Pierre-Adrien 326
Paul Valéry, rue 246
Peking (also called Beijing) 286
Perriand, Charlotte 272, 276, 279
Peru 246, 250, 325
Peter the Great, Emperor of Russia
    46
Petyarre, Anna 369, 370
Pfeiffer, Fanny von 258
Pfyffer d'Althishofen, Louis 32
Philip III, King of Spain 230
Philip IV, King of Spain 230
Philip V, King of Spain 234
Pierre, Comte de 144
Pillet-Will, Comte Frédéric 272
Poland 158, 162
Pollet, Joseph Michel-Ange 14
Pontalba, Célestin Delfau, Baron de
    176
Pontalba, Joseph Delfau, Baron de
    176
Pontalba, Baronesse de (Michaela
    Leonarda Almonester y Roxas,
    commonly known as) 176, 178,
    183, 187
Porto 345, 346
Portugal 332, 335, 340, 345
Pottey, Willem 88
Prado, museum 230
Prelle, manufacture of 82
Procaccini, Andrea 230
Proust, Marcel 162, 194, 196, 228,
    238, 246, 332, 340
Prouvé, Jean 272, 279
Prussia 13
Pueyrredón, Prilidiano 304, 308
Pukumani, community 364

Q

Qatar *218, 222*
Qing, dynasty *286*
Quirin Jahn, John *23*

R

Raquin, Octave *272*
Raveaux, Étienne *110*
Raymond Poincaré, avenue *314*
Rembrandt, (Rembrandt Harmenszoon
  van Rijn) *146*
Renoir, Auguste *353*
Richelieu, Armand Jean du Plessis,
  Cardinal and Duc de *10*
Riedberger, Jacques-Henri *272*
Rigo, Michel *68*
Rijksmuseum, museum *90*
Robert, Hubert *67*
Robirosa, Josefina *304, 308*
Rodin, Auguste *212*
Rodin, museum *178*
Rohan, Duc de *32*
Rohault de Fleury, Charles *218*
Romania *194, 196*
Rosas, family, goldsmiths *345*
Rothschild, Baronne Berthe Claire de,
  and Princesse de Wagram *228*
Rothschild, Edmond James de, Baron
  176, 178
Rothschild, Maurice de, Baron *178*
Rouvre, family *286*
Rubé, Auguste Alfred *18*
Russia *46, 50*

S

Sábato, Ernesto *308*
Sagan, prince de *162*
Saint-Dominique, rue *158, 194, 212*
Saint-Petersburg, manufacture of *48*
Saint-Saëns, Camille *212*
Sakakura, Junzo *272*
Sandrié, Gilles Hiérosme *144*
Sanson, Ernest *258*
Santa Barbara, royal manufacture of
  228, 238
Scotland *118*
Seckel, Christophe *23*
Ségur, Anne Madeleine Louise,
  Marquise de *32*
Ségur, Joseph-Alexandre, Vicomte de *32*
Ségur, Maréchal de *32*
Seidler, Harry *364, 366*
Seillière, Achille, Baron *162*
Seine, river *10, 18, 23, 62, 67, 364,
  366, 369*
Seligmann, Jacques *162*
Sergent, René *322, 350*
Sert, José Maria *230, 234, 240*
Sert, Misia *230*
Sèvres, porcelain manufacture of *10, 23,
  250, 264, 266, 332*
Short, William *183*
Shyam, Jangarh Singh *353*
Sieyès, Abbé *158*
Sívori, Eduardo *308*
Slaska, porcelain manufacture of *170*
Smith, Karryne *366*
Soleure *32*

Spain *13, 32, 228, 240*
Spencer Churchill, Charles, Duke of
  Marlborough *350*
Spontini, rue *332*
Steinbach , Jules *350*
Stieler, Joseph Karl *62*
Stoullig, Charles *314*
Stuart de Rothesay, Lord Charles *106*
Stuart de Rothesay, Lady Elizabeth *106*
Surène, rue de *144*
Switzerland *32, 34, 36*
Szenes, Arpad *336*

T

Tagus, river *335*
Talleyrand-Périgord, Jeanne de
  (born Seillière) *162*
Terreiro do Paço *335*
Thomire, Pierre-Philippe *64, 70, 106,
  110*
Tilsitt, rue de *144, 218*
Tiwi, people *364*
Tjungurrayi, Helicopter *369*
Tokuda, Yasokichi *272*
Tokyo, palais de *162*
Torcy, Jean-Baptiste Colbert,
  Marquis de *62*
Tourzel, Augustine de,
  Duchesse des Cars *46*
Tourzel, Marquise de *46*
Troy, Jean-François de *124, 127*

U

United Kingdom of Great Britain
  and Northern Ireland *102, 110*
United States of America *176, 178,
  188, 325, 350, 353, 366*
Utopia, community *370*

V

Valéry, Paul *194, 203*
Vallotton, Félix *34*
Vanderbilt, Consuelo, Duchess of
  Marlborough (married Jacques Balsan)
  350
Vanderbilt, family *353*
Vanderbilt, William Kissam *350*
Varanasi *353, 354, 360*
Varenne, rue de *58, 124*
Vargas Llosa, Mario *246*
Vauchelet, Théophile Auguste *10*
Velde, Willem Van de (the Younger) *97*
Versailles, château de *124, 194, 196*
Victoria, Queen *102, 106, 114*
Vieira da Silva, Maria Helena *336*
Vienna *366*
Villeroy, Gabriel Louis François
  de Neufville, Duc de *62*
Villiers, George *102*
Visconti, Louis *105, 118, 176*
Vista Alegre, porcelain factory *335, 345*

W

Wagner, Richard *76*
Wagram, Prince de, *228*
Waldegg, château de *32*
Walpole, Horatio *88, 158*
Washington, George *176*

Watson, Arthur K. *178*
Wellington, Arthur Wellesley, Duke of
  105, 106
Whitworth, Lord Charles *102*
Widor, Charles-Marie *212*
Wieniawski, Henryk *170*
Williams Hope, William *158, 162*
Winterhalter, Franz Xaver *18, 102*

Y

Yamamoto, Izuru *283*
Yin-Yang, *288, 290*
Yixing *288, 295*
Ysendyck, Antoon Van *149*

Z

Zanzibar, island of *218*